ADVANCE PRAISE FOR *YOU ONLY LIVE ONCE*

"Are you wondering, "Is this all there is?" Head to the nearest bookstore and buy a copy of *You Only Live Once: Create the Life You Want.* This book helps you explore the question, "Am I living a life that will lead to regrets?" and then shares specific suggestions on how you can make your life what you want it to be now, not someday. Highly recommended."

~Sam Horn, The Intrigue Expert and Author of *POP!* and *SerenDestiny*

"*You Only Live Once: Create the Life You Want* strikes at the heart of how to live an authentic life, step by precious step. Don't just read it—live it!"

~David Fox, M.D., Author of *Comfort, Healing, and Joy: Secrets to Living a Magnificent Life*

"*You Only Live Once* calls us to reexamine our lives through a different lens. Deirdre offers a solid roadmap to helping us create a life based on what is meaningful, fulfilling and important for each of us. I highly recommend this book!"

~Claudette Rowley, Certified Professional Co-active Coach, Consultant and Author of *Embrace Your Brilliance: How to Align Yourself with Your Unique Potential*

"*You Only Live Once: Create the Life You Want* can be anything from a loud wake-up call to a gentle reminder that there may still be ways to make your life even better. A recommended read for everyone."

~Noelle Boc, Librarian, Tewksbury Public Library, Tewksbury, Massachusetts

"We all come up against life challenges. Many times I have wished for a step-by-step plan to guide me through. When you find that guidance in a book it becomes more valuable than gold. How precious to find this book, *You Only Live Once: Create the Life You Want.* I am sending it to all of my friends and clients."

~Maya Balle, Master Certified Coach, Certified Professional Co-active Coach

"*You Only Live Once: Create the Life You Want* sends a message that we should all be living each day as if it was our last and to reach for what we want out of life! I highly recommend this book to anyone who is looking to live life to the fullest and to learn how to get there."

~Linda Belan, Owner of Your Outsource Solutions, LLC

"As a life-long learner, I could not put this book down! It helped me to recognize that I need to stop the madness of my schedule and make room for "me time" if I am ever to get what I want from life."

~Nancy Mara-Aldrich, Human Resources and Legal Consultant

"When I read *You Only Live Once: Create the Life You Want,* I recognized myself immediately as the chronic multi-tasker. This book helped me to return to the pleasure of doing one thing at a time, and doing it well."

~Michele O'Brien, Executive Director, Law For All

"At first I found myself challenged by the book's thesis but as I read on, I was increasingly impressed not only with Deirdre's wisdom, but also with her compassionate approach to aspects of life most of us overlook. She builds a wonderful case for embracing what the new age thinkers have been telling us for years—"slow down and smell the roses"—and goes on to tell us in practical, doable steps, exactly how. I already have friends and clients to whom I plan to recommend this book!"

~Marilyn Edelson, MCC, Business and Career Coach, Speaker, and Author of *Values-based Coaching: A Guide for Social Workers and other Human Service Professionals*

"*You Only Live Once: Create the Life You Want* is a clear and concise primer on realizing your desired personal and professional goals. This book successfully redefines the daily struggle of being driven to achieve unfulfilling, task-oriented objectives, but instead seek goals which exalt happiness, enlightenment, and personal peace. This book is a step-by-step guide populated with inspirational anecdotes and exercises that act as waypoints to get you started, keep you focused, and keep you on track."

~Kevin Dufour, Esq.

"After starting to read *You Only Live Once*, I immediately became excited. It is so well written and inspirational that you want to start your new life right away. I am ready for the work it will take to make this happen. With Deirdre's careful guidance I feel like I can do anything!"

-Alison Gleason Petersen, Landscape Designer and Mother of Two

"Wow, a great read! I felt like I was sitting in a room having a conversation with a good friend."

-Nicole Kjellquist, Paramedic, Exeter Hospital, Exeter NH

"Reading Deirdre's book, I'm reminded of what I want to focus on to get a better balance in my life. I could relate to the stories in the book and found the exercises empowering. This book gave me the tools I needed."

-Rosemary White, Financial Planner

"You Only Live Once: Create the Life You Want is a book for those who are ready to sit with themselves and reflect on their goals, desires and what ifs. The exercises are thought- and action-provoking in a positive and inspiring manner."

-Eileen Weir, Teacher, Boston Public Schools

"A LIFE-CHANGING BOOK! *You Only Live Once* focuses on helping people empower themselves and live enriching, juicy, full lives. Filled with heartwarming stories and examples and meaningful quotes, as well as inspiring life lessons and helpful exercises, this book enables individuals to find their purpose and take their lives to a whole new level. As a coach who promotes joy and life balance in my own practice, this book will be a valuable resource for my clients and a special gift to anyone going through a transition or wishing to create the life they truly want."

-K.C. Christensen-Lang, President, Happiness Is…,
Co-author of *Speaking of Success*

You Only Live *Once*

Create the Life You Want

An award-winning life coach guides you through her proven five-step program for dramatically improving your life, starting today

Deirdre M. McEachern, MCC

Love Your Life Publishing, Inc., 7127 Mexico Road Suite 121
Saint Peters, MO 63376
www.LoveYourLifePublishing.com
publisher@LoveYourLifePublishing.com

ISBN: 978-1-934509-40-1
Library of Congress Control Number: 2011927186

Printed in the United States of America
Cover and Internal Design by: www.Cyanotype.ca

First Printing: 2011

Oct. 2011
Cynthia & Alec,
Live life to the fullest!
Love, Margaret

DEDICATION

For Aidan and Maeve.
May you always create the life you want.

ACKNOWLEDGMENTS

This book would not have been possible without the advice, expertise, support and talent of many people. First and foremost, I wish to thank my many clients who appear on these pages. They generously shared their stories for the benefit of others. I am honored to have had the privilege of working with them and am extremely grateful for their willingness to be part of this book.

I also must thank my early team of readers who bravely pored over an unfinished manuscript and offered detailed and constructive feedback: Michele O'Brien, Deborah Coffey, Eileen Weir, K. C. Christensen-Lang, Kelly Hevel, Gary France, Eileen White, Vera Scanlon, Claudette Rowley, Andrea Novakowski, Jean Benda, Aimee Campbell, Jennifer Zaslow and Elizabeth Dice. I would be remiss if I did not also thank Sam Horn, who guided me like a trusted teacher, educating me with her wisdom, experience and practical advice about the book publishing industry.

I will be forever indebted to Pamela Angulo, an extremely talented editor who applied her dedication, talent and finesse to ensure that the words and the nuances of my coaching process were captured perfectly on the written page. I am also grateful for the professional expertise, support and encouragement of editor Amy Scott, who laid the solid foundation of the earlier version of this book, and Louise Gordon, my first proofreader and a fan who encouraged me to bring this book to the world.

I must also thank Sarah Barrie, the talented artist who created the wonderful cover and interior layout for this book. She captured the essence of its message so perfectly. Gwen Hoffnagle, a highly skilled proofreader and editor-at-large, deserves my heartfelt thanks as well for seeing to it that the final version was absolutely perfect.

I deeply thank my family, friends and coaching colleagues for believing in me so much that I believed in myself, most notably, Henri and Margaret Dufour, Duncan and Patti McEachern, Kevin and Michele Dufour, Henri Dufour, Paul Beaulieu, Kim Ky, Alan Rintoul, Colm Rogers, Nicole Kjellquist, Noelle Boc, Michele Perera, Eli Holmes, John Montague, Dayan Goodsir-Cullen, Carol Reichenthal, Claudette Rowley, Marilyn Edelson, Maya Balle, Ariane Cherbuliez, Tammy Gooler-Loeb, Mino Sullivan, Connie Adkins and so many others who have been supportive of me and my work, directly or indirectly.

A very special thank-you goes out to Katie Pelletier and Kiersten Palmer. Their extraordinary skill, creativity and warmth with my children made the fruition of this book possible.

Sincere and heartfelt thanks to Lynne Klippel, my publisher, whose expert guidance has supported me every step of the way and made the process fun and easy.

Last but certainly not least, this book never would have come into being without the love and constant encouragement of Joe McEachern, the most kind and supportive husband any author could ask for. Thank you, Joe, for walking with me on this journey of many miles.

CONTENTS

WHY THIS BOOK IS RIGHT FOR YOU

Let the beauty of what you love, be what you do. –RUMI

Now that you've picked up this book, you may be flipping through the pages, trying to determine whether it's appropriate for you and your current situation. The following sections explain why it—and the five-step You Only Live Once (YOLO) program—is perfect for you, right now.

You Want More from Life

Do you feel like there must be more in store for you than what you have now? That your talent, time or effort is wasted? That you are not meeting your potential? No matter what your complaints or where you are on your journey, the YOLO program can help you resolve the issues that make you feel frustrated, unfulfilled, fed up, held back, stuck, restrained or trapped—whether those feelings stem from your job, relationship, living situation, personal health, a long-elusive goal or something else.

It is impossible to be truly happy with your life if one or more than one aspect of your life drains you, leaving no energy for the activities and people you would normally enjoy. Because the YOLO program systematically addresses *every* aspect of your life, each area will receive the attention it deserves so you can achieve the life you want. Throughout this process, you will learn to use powerful techniques for looking inward and asking yourself questions that reveal your truest, most compelling answers.

The YOLO program is not a quick fix, but a long-term solution, because it treats the whole you—a person with many aspects—and teaches you techniques that can be taken out into the world and used wherever and whenever they might be needed.

You Want a New Career or Job

If your most pressing area of dissatisfaction is work, you're not alone. At the national level, fifty-five percent of Americans—across all ages and income brackets—are unhappy with their jobs.[1] Most of my clients initially come to me with work issues, wanting to significantly alter or completely change their careers. These kinds of problems affect people profoundly because so much of our time and identities are intertwined with work.

As a life coach, I have observed that job dissatisfaction tends to be an indicator of dissatisfaction in other aspects of life. For example, seventy-five percent of my career-change clients decide to improve another life area after addressing their career issues. The good news is that resolving work-related issues frees up emotional energy, creativity and practical resources for the other areas of life that may also need attention.

1. The Conference Board. 2010. *U.S. Job Satisfaction at Lowest Level in Two Decades* (Press/News Archive, January 5). New York, NY: The Conference Board. www.conference-board.org/press/pressdetail.cfm?pressid=3820

The YOLO program makes satisfaction in work—and ultimately, in life—legitimate and achievable by offering a clear, structured path to change in all areas of your life. It will not teach you how to create a winning résumé or identify your ideal career (skills you might learn from one-on-one career coaching). Instead, you will discover what makes you feel fulfilled, which aspects of life are interconnected and how small changes can achieve dramatic results. You may choose to make a major shift in your career or simply fine-tune where or how you work. Or you may integrate your work life and personal life in a unique way that supports your overall happiness. The ultimate goal is for you to achieve a career or job that leaves you the time, energy and freedom to pursue all of the important areas of your life to their fullest, most satisfying potential.

You Want an Expert Who Understands

As your guide on this journey, I offer more than a decade of experience helping thousands of people dramatically improve their lives. Because we won't be working together in person, this book acts as my proxy, guiding and encouraging you all the way through the five-step YOLO program. Working your way through this book is the closest you can come to working with me without making an appointment.

Even though I love my current life and being a Master Certified Life Coach, I know what it's like to feel dissatisfied and discouraged (as you'll learn in the stories that appear throughout this book). I also know that making a dramatic life change for the better is both possible and within reach.

Perhaps not coincidentally, career dissatisfaction started me on my own journey to my ideal life. To help you understand where I have been, let's flash back to the beginning of the path that led me to where I am today.

A few years after college, I had a temporary administrative job that paid the bills—barely—but was unfulfilling and not in my field of study or interest. Then a friend convinced me to apply for a permanent position at the small-but-growing software firm where he worked. I applied and was relieved to be hired as the receptionist's assistant. (Yes, that's the assistant *to the* receptionist.*)*

Because I didn't know much about business or computers at the time, I felt lucky to have this entry-level job. Over the next several years I worked hard, learned a lot, and was promoted up the ranks to a director position in which I oversaw a large staff, had a window office and brought home a six-figure salary.

Indeed, I had achieved many peoples' idea of success—power, prestige and money—and you might even be thinking, "Yes, I want that!" For a long time I thought I wanted it, too; then I began to feel burned out, frustrated and unwell. And at what some would consider the peak of my professional career, I decided to walk away and never look back.

I swiveled around in my chair to look out the window. Rather than feeling proud of my eleventh-floor office with a view of the Charles River and enjoying the twinkling lights of Boston at nightfall, I felt trapped in a glass box, being watched from the outside. I thought of all the people out there like me, working late into the night. Why did we bother? Then I asked myself, "What have I been giving up for my slice of the proverbial pie?"

By working so many hours a week, I had been trading away the activities that gave my life meaning, a sense of purpose and good health for a desirable title and an office with a view. Even though I "had it all" as far as many people were concerned, I needed to dramatically change my career—and my life—to become happy, fulfilled and healthy.

Through many trials, tribulations and epiphanies, I left high-tech management, started a life coaching company, created home and work environments that I love, and measurably improved my health and lifestyle in many ways. Change didn't happen overnight or all at once, but I did make it happen. And you can make dramatic changes, too, if you're willing to follow the five-step YOLO program.

You Want a Program That Works

The YOLO program is based on reality—not theory—from my personal experience creating a new life and my professional experience coaching others to do the same. The concepts and exercises have been developed over many years. They have been distilled from a mix of trial-and-error efforts, discoveries, struggles and successes, which include being coached, training to be a life coach, studying personal development, sharing with colleagues and simply observing what works (and what doesn't) with my clients. This book is filled with vignettes about and testimonials from *real people*—me and others—who have worked the YOLO program and whose lives have been changed as a result.

Some of the exercises might take you outside of your comfort zone, but none are beyond your capabilities. How do I know? Because I have worked through every exercise in this book myself—many more than once!—and so have my clients.

You Can Have What You Want!

You deserve to have all the aspects of the life you dream of: joy, happiness, good health, a comfortable home, close relationships, rewarding work, financial stability and plenty of opportunities to enjoy life. Don't worry about the past. If you have been dissatisfied, know that your experience has served a purpose in preparing you for what is to come. The important time is NOW. Gather your hopes and passions and begin a journey in a wonderful new direction. By working with me through the tried-and-true YOLO program, you will break from the past and invent a new future.

If you are ready to make lasting change, **this book will help you dramatically improve your life.** I am always excited about guiding people on the journey of redesigning their lives, and I am excited about guiding you.

Let's get started!

How to Get the Most From This Book

To understand what awaits you, start here. Learn what to expect and how to get maximum benefit from the You Only Live Once program. Then jump right in with some preparatory exercises and test your commitment to yourself.

Wish not so much to live long as to live well.

-Benjamin Franklin

The You Only Live Once (YOLO) program has evolved in response to real lives—mine and my clients'. These tried-and-true techniques have been used for more than a decade in my global coaching practice, and the universal lessons apply to everyone, regardless of age, gender, career, financial status, geography or ethnicity. Every concept, idea and exercise has been validated by people like you—people who were determined, accepted the challenge and, ultimately, dramatically changed their lives. You will meet some of them in these chapters, and I hope that their stories will both inspire you and make your journey easier.

In this book you will:

- Read personal stories of my own life challenges, changes and successes.
- Meet people who have used these five steps to achieve the lives of their dreams.

- Work through the YOLO program and dramatically change your life.
- Learn techniques to continue living the lessons learned as you start your new life.

The exercises may push you into unfamiliar territory, but the results will be well worth it. Keep reading to find out what to expect and how to get started.

Book Overview and Suggestions

The best way to predict the future is to create it.

~Peter Drucker

In this book, I will guide you, like I have guided hundreds of clients before you, through the process of achieving the life you want. You may wish to start a new career; meet a soul mate; move to a new house, city or country; accomplish a personal goal like running a marathon, traveling abroad or creating a masterpiece; or all of the above! Whatever you wish to accomplish, following the proven five-step You Only Life Once program will get you there.

The Chapters

Each step is presented separately, in its own chapter, along with examples and exercises to stimulate and guide you. The five steps are:

- Step 1: Put "Enjoy Life" Back on the Agenda—learn to harness the strategic and health advantages of a happier lifestyle
- Step 2: Go Inward to Find Your Answers—begin to hear and trust your natural wisdom
- Step 3: Design Your Ideal Life—create a detailed plan for your new life

- Step 4: Redefine What It Means to Be Productive—identify what makes your life worth living, then give it precedence

- Step 5: Build Your Self-Confidence—gain the confidence and skills needed to overcome any obstacle to your happiness

Each step builds on the previous one, so please follow the steps in the order in which they are presented. Think of the progression this way: Steps 1 and 2 are preparation (building the core foundational skills necessary for you to effectively complete the later work), Step 3 is planning (mapping out your future life), and Steps 4 and 5 are implementation (learning how to avoid potential obstacles and make your plans reality).

The closing chapter, "Make Your Way in the Real World," provides supportive techniques for putting the lessons from Steps 1 through 5 into practice every day as you follow your vision toward your goals.

To Hire, or Not to Hire (a Coach)

This book is jam-packed with detailed and thought-provoking exercises and is intended to function as your *virtual life coach* all by itself. Be prepared to use it thoroughly. Break the binding, dog-ear the pages, write in the margins and highlight at will. Work through every exercise thoughtfully and completely. And throughout the process, share your insights with at least one reliable person (e.g., a partner, friend or close co-worker). Ask that person to hold you accountable to your objectives, help you brainstorm and celebrate your successes.

However, if you want to make faster progress and have the resources, consider hiring a living, breathing life coach to work through the steps with you. And if you like the idea of working with a real person but have a limited budget, seek out a newly graduated life coach who needs hours for certification and may be willing to support you on a barter, discounted or pro bono basis. (When I began my coaching business, I offered coaching in exchange for all sorts of useful services, such as personal training, web design and printing.) Because the book lays out a tested program, even a new life coach should be able to provide useful assistance.

No matter how you choose to work through the five-step YOLO program, trust this book. Remember, it's your virtual life coach! Be honest with it and do what it asks. If you do, you will be bountifully rewarded with the progress and new life that you want.

Time Considerations

Working through the YOLO program is not difficult, but it does require time and effort. And although reading these chapters may increase your self-knowledge, courage, innovation and determination, simply reading is not enough! Life coaching is an interactive process, and you must complete all the exercises to achieve the successful results you seek.

Approach this book as if it were a continuing education course: For each chapter or step, ensure that you will have quiet, focused and uninterrupted time to read, reflect on and complete the related exercises. Also, please choose a dedicated journal or notebook and keep it with this book. I refer to it as your YOLO journal throughout the book, and you will use it to record your exercises and write down any ideas that resonate with you as you work though the program.

How long should it take to work through the YOLO program? Although you *could* skim through the entire book in an afternoon, please don't! You would cheat yourself out of the full value that it offers, which is permanent, life-improving changes. Do not skip exercises that you perceive as difficult, unimportant or too time-consuming, because those exercises are probably the ones you most need to do! The exercises that you do reluctantly (or procrastinate about) will give you the most vital information about what you want and need in your life. (Avoidance is a common manifestation of *fear* or *limited thinking,* which you need to understand and overcome to create the life you want. These concepts are discussed in depth in Step 5: Build Your Self-Confidence.)

Completing all of the exercises in this book may take a month or more, depending on your determination, stick-to-itiveness and time constraints. You can complete the exercises in Steps 1 and 2 right away and start practicing them in your daily life; however, Steps 3, 4 and 5 (which contain more comprehensive exercises) require deep contemplation and can take a couple of weeks apiece.

No matter how much time you intend to dedicate to this program, your progress will be quicker and more beneficial if you can create quiet, distraction-free time for reading and reflection each time you pick up this book.

> By the way, I've prepared a special guided meditation to support you while you complete the exercises in this book.
> Go to **www.YouOnlyLiveOnceBook.com/readergift**
> and download your free copy.

Preparing for Change

Shooting for the top will bring out the best that's in you.

~Earl Nightingale

When was the last time you thought, "I love my life!" or felt deep contentment—that feeling that everything is right in your world? If you can't remember, then you're in good company. Many of my clients don't like certain aspects of their lives and feel powerless to create the changes they want. What's more, some people I meet in social situations relate the same dreams, year after year, without getting any closer to attaining those dreams. Why? Because they are only talking and wishing, not *doing*. No action follows their words.

Today, for you, things will be different. You will start with action. How? By examining the meanings behind two very personal words that you rarely hear mentioned together, if ever: *daydreams* and *mortality.*

The Power of Daydreams

Being described as "a dreamer" or "lost in daydreams" has never been much of a compliment, but daydreams are not fruitless fantasy. Rather, they are glimpses into your subconscious desires. When you pay attention to them, they point you toward a better life.

The dreaming part is easy. The work lies in deciphering what your dreams are telling you when you return to daily life. A daydream is difficult to analyze when your boss is waiting for a report, the kids have to be picked up or you need to return an important phone call. Complete Exercise 1: Record Daydream Data to help you carve out a moment to take note of and pay attention to what your daydreams have been trying to tell you. It will help you start to identify vital details about the life you wish you were living.

EXERCISE 1:
Record Daydream Data

Carry some paper (a small notepad, a few sticky notes or a blank sheet) and a pencil or pen around with you for a few days. If you are more high-tech than that, please feel free to use your preferred portable electronic note-taking gadget.

→ When you catch yourself daydreaming, jot down a few notes. Here are some questions to guide you:

1. What was your daydream about? Walking hand in hand with someone you love? Performing before a sold-out crowd in an auditorium? Painting a beautiful still life? Sitting in a beach chair on a warm summer's day? Receiving an award?

2. Do you repeatedly travel to a certain location or setting, such as the mountains, when you daydream?

3. If you cannot recall a specific place or event, what was the theme or feeling of your daydream? Freedom? Achievement? Togetherness? Longing?

Copy or paste your notes into your YOLO journal. (You will refer to these insights in Step 1: Put "Enjoy Life" Back on the Agenda, Exercise 4: Identify What Has Been Missing, page 41.)

Mortality and Life Choices

Making dramatic life changes requires making conscious life choices, that is, recognizing what you wish for and then doing what it takes to make it real. When planning an event, you need to know your schedule, right? The same goes for planning your life. You must allocate time for the things that make you happiest.

Let's talk about the concept of time. Sometimes life launches a surprise attack, alerting us to never underestimate time. An unexpected illness or death can be a humbling reminder of how quickly life can change—or even end. Too often, people procrastinate about making even small changes to improve their lives, instead choosing to put them off until they have "more time." Unfortunately, statistics indicate that average life expectancy is much lower than you might think: just under seventy-eight years.[2]

Seventy-seven years doesn't seem long, does it? Most people assume that they will beat the average and live much longer than that. But even though some will, others won't make it past seventy. No matter how old you are, it's time to stop taking life for granted. Don't put off until "someday" what you can do today.

Mortality and death are nobody's favorite discussion topics, but I believe that people can make their best life choices (and create richer lives) after recognizing—even briefly—their mortality. Personal power depends on a healthy awareness of its existence. Here is an account of an experience in which mortality quickly was brought into clear focus:

> *One Christmas just two years into my marriage, my husband Joe came down with a mysterious and debilitating illness. He suffered from high fevers, joint pain and extreme fatigue and was mostly semiconscious. Doctors sent him for blood test after blood test, and as each one ruled out another diagnosis, our anxiety mounted.*

---

2. Arias, Elizabeth. United States Life Tables, 2006. *National Vital Statistics Reports 2010:* Vol. 58, No. 21, p. 2. www.cdc.gov/nchs/data/nvsr/nvsr58/nvsr58_21.pdf

Joe was scheduled for a CT scan on New Year's Eve. While the rest of the world celebrated, we sat in a hospital waiting room and worried. Across the room from us sat an older woman, dressed in a hospital gown just like Joe's.

After a nurse took the woman for her test, the woman's companion announced, "She's my best friend" to no one in particular, yet to the whole room. "She's been my best friend for forty years," he added, with a thick accent. "We came to this country together and now we have five children." His voice was heavy with sadness. He clearly was afraid of losing her.

"I hope she's going to be okay," I offered, unsure of what else to say. Then I looked at Joe and prayed that his condition wasn't life-threatening. Our life together was only getting started.

A few days later, Joe's test results were delivered: all clear. Even though he remained ill for another six weeks, he recovered completely from what was ultimately diagnosed as a rare virus. But this harrowing experience—our stress, so many unknowns and witnessing the fear of the man we had shared a waiting room with—taught me to never take for granted the time I have with my loved ones.

Perhaps you have already learned this lesson. Most people feel, at some moment in life, like they are on the verge of losing someone vitally important. In day-to-day life, it is natural to assume that partners, family and best friends will always be there—but that assumption is not based on reality. When a loved one's mortality becomes painfully apparent to you, will you wish you had chosen to spend more time with that person? And when your day comes to depart this earth, will you look back and wish you had spent more time enjoying life? If you think your answer could be yes to either of these questions, this book will help you create healthy, life-enhancing habits now so you can have wonderful memories—instead of regrets—later.

Living in fear of death is no way to live. However, being realistic and practical about your mortality can give you that little shock you need to move from inaction to action. Complete Exercise 2: How Long *Do* I Have? to get an idea about how long *your* life might be. When you begin to look at your remaining lifespan as a budget of years, days or experiences, you will make more powerful decisions about how you live your life each day.

EXERCISE 2:

How Long *Do* I Have?

Although no tool can predict the age at which you will die, completing this exercise can give you a sense that life is finite and that you should cherish the time you have and use it wisely. With the realization that time cannot be stopped, you will be more motivated to dramatically change your life and start to create the life you want, immediately.

→ First, estimate your life expectancy using a life expectancy calculator. Financial planners and life insurance companies are more than happy to provide such a tool for free. Or, type "life expectancy calculator" into any Internet search engine to find an online version. (Note: If you don't have access to such a tool, simply use the average life expectancy of seventy-seven years. And if you are already older than seventy-seven, sit back and smirk, knowing that you have beaten the odds!)

Next, from your calculated life expectancy, subtract your current age. The result is how many years you most likely have left to live; make a note of it in your YOLO journal.

Finally, define your remaining life in terms of a number of important milestones or favorite activities: how many birthdays left to celebrate, how many holidays left to spend with family or how many summers left to walk the beach. List them in your YOLO journal to remind yourself that mortality is a tangible rather than an abstract concept.

Are You Ready?

Thinking is easy, acting difficult, and to put one's thoughts into action, the most difficult thing in the world.

–Johann Wolfgang von Goethe

While you work through the five-step YOLO program, some exercises may push you out of your comfort zone; however, a little discomfort is necessary to create long-term, sustainable change. You also will need to commit yourself to this program in terms of time and effort. When you do, your reward will be a dramatically more fulfilling, enriched and happy life, and you can start your journey right now.

Exercise 3: The Commitment Contract is a pledge to yourself. Are you ready to work hard to achieve what you truly desire? Read each statement carefully, and circle your truthful answer. If all of your answers are yes, then I am pleased to be your guide on your journey to the life you want.

However, if any statements make you hesitate, or if your honest answer to any statement is no, then stop; you are not ready for this program right now. A long-held fear could be holding you back. Please work with a life coach or other professional to break free of this fear, and when you are ready, come back to take full advantage of this life-changing process.

As soon as you have successfully completed this exercise confirming your commitment to yourself and the YOLO program, turn the page and begin with Step 1: Put "Enjoy Life" Back on the Agenda. Your future awaits!

EXERCISE 3:

The Commitment Contract
You Only Live Once Agreement

I, ______________________, am committed to reading You Only Live Once: Create the Life You Want and completing all of the included exercises. I commit to making dramatic changes in my life, reaching my goals and living the life I want.

I hereby attest that:

I feel trapped; I want more from life but don't know how to go after it.	Yes	No
I am ready and willing to learn how to achieve the life I want.	Yes	No

I agree to use this book to best meet my needs by:

• Being honest with myself about my motivations	Yes	No
• Creating time to read this book and do the exercises	Yes	No
• Asking others for help with the program when needed	Yes	No
• Being accountable for the actions I commit to	Yes	No

I give this book permission to:

• Challenge me with powerful questions and exercises	Yes	No
• Ask me to take action when needed	Yes	No
• Provide deep inquiries for me to consider thoroughly	Yes	No

I will continue to plan and take actions based on my insights from this book even after I have finished reading it.	Yes	No
I will share my ongoing success with family and friends.	Yes	No
I am ready to begin the You Only Live Once program today.	Yes	No

Signature_______________________________________ Date:_______

Put "Enjoy Life" Back on the Agenda

DON'T GO THROUGH LIFE FEELING UNHAPPY AND UNFULFILLED; LIFE IS TOO SHORT! LEARN TO WEIGH THE VALUE OF THE THINGS YOU HAVE TO DO SO YOU CAN PUT YOUR HAPPINESS AT THE TOP OF YOUR TO-DO LIST.

When you discover that your lifestyle is controlling you rather than you controlling it, you know you have a problem.

–BRYAN ROBINSON

Terms Used in This Chapter

perpetual progress mind-set: a sense of cultural pressure to continually achieve more in each day, week, month, year or life

mental agenda: a personal to-do list that is constantly updated in your mind and used to keep track of everything that needs to get done—work, appointments, goals, errands, social obligations, family responsibilities, hobbies—and tends to command full attention

mental exhaustion: temporarily feeling drained, overwhelmed, unhappy and, eventually, disillusioned

multitasking: doing more than one task or thought at a time—and thinking ahead to the next thing before finishing what you're doing right now

monotasking: doing just one thing (task or thought) at a time

coasting: taking a break from your mental agenda or to-do list to simply enjoy the moment

You have already taken an important preparatory step toward dramatically changing your life. Completing Exercise 2: How Long *Do* I Have? helped you develop an awareness of your mortality, giving you the necessary perspective for working on Step 1: Put "Enjoy Life" Back on the Agenda.

This step is not about understanding the *quantity* of days you have left but improving the *quality* of each and every day. To get a better idea about what this means, let's take a look at today's typical lifestyle.

What's in a Day?

An early morning walk is a blessing for the whole day.

–Henry David Thoreau

Most people in the United States today are hooked into what I call the *perpetual progress mind-set*—a societal pressure they feel to continually achieve. This pressure drives people toward all sorts of personal goals, like being a better parent, partner, child or person; getting a promotion at work; or becoming more physically fit. However, if not kept in perspective—in other words, if this pressure isn't balanced with activities that bring happiness—it can be exhausting.

To keep up with the demands of the perpetual progress mind-set, each person maintains a *mental agenda,* a sort of ongoing personal to-do list that is constantly updated in one's mind. It is how you keep track of things that need to get done—work, appointments, goals, errands, social obligations, family responsibilities and even hobbies and other fun activities. It is used to organize and structure your life. A mental agenda is necessary, but constant attention to it, without breaks, can be emotionally draining.

Imagine reading a long book in very small print … eventually your vision gets so blurry that you have to give your eyes a rest. The same is true for your mind.

If it doesn't get a break once in a while, your thinking gets blurry. The continual focus on progress and its daily demands eventually leads to a temporary emotional state referred to as *mental exhaustion,* in which you feel drained, overwhelmed, unhappy and disillusioned.

You know that you are mentally exhausted when you hear yourself saying (or thinking) things like, "There has to be more to life than this!" "What was I looking for in this closet?" or "Where on earth did I put my car keys?" You may notice yourself operating on autopilot, still getting things done but without thinking about *what* you are doing or even *why* you are doing it.

The experience of Craig, a husband and father in his late thirties, is a good example of mental exhaustion.[3] Craig attended my workshop on work–life balance called Making the Most of Your Time, which his professional association offered as part of their leadership development program. In this workshop, participants' true priorities are identified, then strategies are created to incorporate those priorities into their everyday schedules.

> *Craig was upset that he had only a few minutes to spend with his two preschool-aged daughters after he got home from work each day. "I always used to take them to visit our neighbor's ponies in the evenings," he explained, his voice tinged with guilt, regret and sadness. "They loved bringing carrots to feed the ponies!" He explained that the business he owned had grown so much that he had to work overtime just to keep up with the paperwork.*
>
> *Achieving one simple, uncomplicated goal—getting home earlier in the evening—would dramatically improve Craig's quality of life. But because he was mentally exhausted, he could not figure out how to make it happen. Luckily, he knew what was important to him and, in his gut, recognized that he needed to make a change.*

3. All names have been changed throughout the book to protect client confidentiality.

> *We brainstormed briefly about creative ways Craig could afford to hire part-time help to handle the paperwork so that he could leave work earlier. To keep his new priority at the top of his mental agenda, he resolved to put doodles of carrots on his desk, near his computer, and in his day planner. It was an eye-catching reminder and a humorous play on the idea of the proverbial carrot-and-stick approach. After all, his ultimate goal of running a successful business was to provide for and be able to spend quality time with his family.*

What happened to Craig happens to so many people. Personal priorities get pushed to the bottom of the mental agenda after professional and other responsibilities. By attending the workshop and then working with me afterward, Craig was able to break out of his status quo. He called me a few weeks later to share how happy he was to be enjoying fun evenings feeding the ponies and creating life-long memories with his two young daughters again.

Creative solutions to work–life balance problems may seem obvious to those around you, but when you are mentally exhausted you are unable to find answers, make clear decisions, express yourself and stay in touch with what matters most. To make matters worse, you cannot see that you need a break, so you keep trying to make progress on your mental agenda, thereby trapping yourself in a vicious cycle.

If you feel drained by mental exhaustion, don't worry; the You Only Live Once (YOLO) program will help you simplify and regain your energy so you can make progress on the tasks that are important to you, one step at a time. Complete Exercise 4: Identify What Has Been Missing to help you reconnect with the people or activities you wish were in your day-to-day life.

EXERCISE 4:

Identify What Has Been Missing

What have you been complaining about missing? When you hear yourself saying, "I used to do that all the time," but now can't seem to find the time, what does that mean? (I often hear this comment about exercising, taking time for creative activities and spending time with important people who have fallen out of touch.)

→ Ask your life coach, partner or friend for about ten or fifteen minutes of their time. Together, brainstorm what you wish you had more time for this week. (For some ideas, refer back to your notes from Exercise 1: Record Daydream Data.) Continue to brainstorm longer, if necessary.

Make a detailed list of these ideas in your YOLO journal so you can refer back to them in Exercise 27: Examine Your Home Productivity.

Multitask Mayhem

Hurry is not "of" the devil; Hurry "is" the devil.

-C. G. Jung

The pressure felt from the perpetual progress mind-set leads to *multitasking*—doing more than one thing at a time—and always thinking ahead to the next thing before finishing what's in process right now in order to get through your mental agenda as quickly as possible. Some forms of multitasking are: eating lunch while checking email, talking on the phone while driving and checking a personal calendar while waiting in line at the store. Multitasking is done at work, at home and even in social lives. We multitask in an effort to get ahead on our mental agendas and gain precious free time for ourselves. But as it turns out, multitasking actually takes longer and drains our energy in the process.

The Ugly Truth of "Busy-ness"

Have you ever lost your train of thought or made a wrong turn while talking on the phone and driving? Here's why: "Studies conducted by the National Institutes of Health showed that different parts of the brain are activated during certain tasks. When people try to do multiple activities at once—such as drive and talk on a cell phone—metabolic activity decreases in both parts of the brain, resulting in poor task completion and lowered efficiency. To make matters worse, when the brain becomes stressed from overload, other parts of the body release stress hormones, like adrenaline. Prolonged release of these hormones takes a physical toll on the body in the form of poor sleep, depression and anxiety."[4]

Research also indicates that the elevated stress levels caused by a busy multitasking lifestyle weaken the immune system and lead to serious conditions such as heart disease, ulcers and hypertension. According to Dr. John Sladky, a neurologist at Emory University, "Behavior that results in stress will result in a whole range of 21st-century diseases."[5]

Clearly, too much multitasking, and the resulting mental overload, are not healthy. Yet people continue to pride themselves on how much they can do at once and how long they can continue without taking a break. Have you ever heard yourself brag, "I have so much to do, but I work better under pressure" or "I haven't had a real vacation in years?" Uh-huh, I used to say that, too. It's the ego talking. Some people like to feel important and as if their continual effort and multitasking are urgent and invaluable. Although it may be true sometimes, it isn't true *all* the time.

4. Anderson, Virginia. 2003. Too Much to Do. *Atlanta Journal-Constitution,* Nov. 18.

5. Anderson 2003.

A quick Internet search on the phrase "too busy" will lead you to dozens of articles from around the world about how the perpetual progress mind-set and its resulting multitasking is making people so busy that ultimately, some things aren't getting done at all! According to popular media, even leisure time is busy. People appear to be too busy to vote, pray, exercise, sleep, breathe, feed the dog ... you name it.

John de Graaf, author of *Affluenza*[6] and founder of Take Back Your Time Day (www.timeday.org), notes: "Stress is now endemic to life. Home and family lives mirror the frenzied productivity that fills workplaces. Children carry appointment calendars; many are now chained to schedules that used to be reserved for CEOs. Even neglect and abandonment of pets is on the rise, as people have less time for them."[7]

To make matters worse, research shows that when this multitasking lifestyle is passed on to kids, the associated poor health conditions go along with it. Children who are overscheduled, put into competitive situations at early ages and overstimulated by battery-operated toys and mediacentric activities don't have enough time to relax, play and just be kids. Doctors report seeing increasing numbers of children with what used to be considered adult health conditions related to stress and anxiety, such as obesity and type 2 diabetes.

The Antidote: Happiness

The "busy-ness" problem is widespread, if not pandemic. Thankfully, some folks have been working on a solution. *New Scientist* magazine reports, "The study of happiness, formerly the preserve of philosophers, academics and therapists has

---

6. de Graaf, John, David Wann, and Thomas H. Naylor in association with Redefining Progress. 2001. *Affluenza: The All-Consuming Epidemic (*1st edition). San Francisco, CA: Berrett-Koehler Publishers.
7. de Graaf, John. no date. *Short on Time? Take Yours Back!* www.newdream.org/newsletter/tbytd.php, accessed Jan. 15, 2004.

become a new discipline."[8] In fact, the desire to figure out how to return to a more meaningful, happy existence has become so strong that you can now find professors of happiness at leading universities and quality-of-life institutes the world over, as well as many research papers published on the subject.

Even national governments are starting to recognize the importance of happiness. The Prime Minister of Great Britain's Strategy Unit published a sixty-four-page paper entitled *Life Satisfaction.*[9] Around the same time, the government of Bhutan—a country about the size of Switzerland nestled in the eastern Himalayas—boldly declared itself more concerned with gross national happiness than gross national product. What a wonderful declaration!

Meanwhile, many grassroots social movements have been established to support the pursuit of happier lives: the widespread simple living movement, John de Graaf's Take Back Your Time Day, and Joe Robinson's Work to Live approach to sustainable performance (taught in his book of the same name), to name a few. The rapid growth of life coaching is another indicator of this growing awareness.

This shift is heartening, but why doesn't anyone feel better? Why do you still need a book like this one to help you create a life you love? Because individuals have become so used to the pressure of the perpetual progress mind-set and so accustomed to living strictly by their mental agenda that their emotional circuits are too frazzled to give personal happiness the importance it deserves. **People are connected to getting things done and disconnected from what makes them happy.** One person at a time, we need to find our way to the path that leads to the life we really want.

---

8. Bond, Michael. 2003. The Pursuit of Happiness. *New Scientist,* Oct. 4.
9. Donovan, Nick, and David Halpern, with Richard Sargeant. 2002. *Life Satisfaction: The State of Knowledge and Implications for Government.* London, UK: Cabinet Office Strategy Unit, December. www.cabinetoffice.gov.uk/media/cabinetoffice/strategy/assets/paper.pdf

It's important to be aware of this cultural pressure of perpetual progress, look critically at your own mental agenda, and deliberately and regularly give yourself a break from the perpetual progress mind-set so you can reconnect with the feelings, events and attitudes that make your life worth living.

Happiness is a subjective feeling—and an elusive one, many people would add. Because it is so personal, it cannot be defined by one person for another. It may even be the case that two people in the same time and place have completely different experiences. Here's an example from my life:

> *From my front porch, I can look out over a tidal river. Sometimes, very early in the morning, I see recreational fishermen casting from their boats. Their voices carry over the water, and I am always amused by how thrilled they sound in the early dawn. They truly love what they are doing. I, on the other hand, much prefer to enjoy the view and my aromatic mug of coffee.*

The point is that to love your life, you must know what makes *your* heart sing. Not your neighbor's heart or even your partner's heart, but yours.

Complete Exercise 5: Enjoy Life, Today to start reprioritizing your to-do list and putting the activities you daydream about at the top. Doing what you enjoy will provide personally fulfilling respite from your day-to-day obligations and help protect you from mental exhaustion.

EXERCISE 5:

Enjoy Life, Today

The essence of Step 1: Put "Enjoy Life" Back on the Agenda is to learn to make normal, necessary progress in your daily life (like work, errands and self- or family-care tasks) while also enjoying much-deserved moments when you can do something that makes you happy. Rearranging your daily priorities does not necessarily mean that you will drop out of society and lollygag all day; it just means making a little room for your happiness along with your obligations.

→ Start by making your to-do list for today, listing all the tasks on your mental agenda in your YOLO journal. For each item, ask yourself the following questions:

1. Must I complete this task today? Can I do it another day?

2. Am I really the only one who can accomplish this task? Can I delegate it to someone else?

After you have reached the end of your list, revise it according to your answers to the following questions:

3. What do I wish were at the top of my to-do list in a perfect world? (Refer back to the list that you created in Exercise 4: Identify What Has Been Missing for ideas.)

4. How much time can I carve out to make that activity (even some condensed version of it) a reality on my agenda today?

Next comes the most important question:

5. When will I do it?

Make an appointment with yourself and write yourself a reminder—on a sticky note, your calendar or your actual to-do list for the day—as a written commitment to yourself. Do not remove or erase the reminder until you have given yourself this overdue gift.

Then ask yourself one final question, and adjust your plans for the day accordingly:

6. What might get in the way of keeping this commitment to myself? How can I plan ahead now to avoid it getting in the way? (For example, do you need to arrange a play date for the kids or tell your boss you need to leave early?)

Enjoy what it feels like to do something that you really wanted to do!

Why Slower Is Better

We have so few occasions built into our contemporary lives where slowing down and reflecting occurs. Yet this is where restorative, spiritual change and inner guidance frequently takes place.

~Lynn Robinson

When talking about busy lifestyles, it's important to differentiate between being productive (which is good) and being frazzled (which is unhealthy). Feeling productive is energizing, whereas feeling frazzled is exhausting.

It is important to remember, anxiety caused by the desire to make perpetual progress by checking off items on your mental agenda can take over your senses, steal vitality and joy from your life, and drive you into the ground.

Wake-Up Call

For some people, it takes a life-altering event to force them out of the perpetual progress mind-set and away from their mental agenda. That's what happened to me many years ago when I was still working in the high-tech industry. I never would have questioned my lifestyle if a serious medical scare hadn't forced me to see it in a new light.

Do you remember the whirlwind Tasmanian devil from the classic Bugs Bunny cartoons? That's how I used to live. I took great pride in my ability to operate while spinning at maximum speed, often on the verge of losing control. I was overbooked, stretched to my limit, and usually running fifteen minutes late. I worked long hours. I organized social events. I jumped for the phone whenever it rang and always was in the middle of some self-improvement project. I ran from one activity or obligation to the next—professionally and *personally—and rarely came up for air. The amount of adrenaline required to live this way kept me buzzing along, but things happened too fast for me to really enjoy them. Making perpetual progress was like a game I played with myself, to see how much I could accomplish on my mental agenda each day.*

Then one morning at work I noticed my pulse was racing. I was scared and had trouble catching my breath, so I went to the emergency room. After many tests, I was told I had a hole in my heart, and that it needed to be closed, necessitating open-heart surgery. Whoa! My mind raced. I was in complete panic. What if I died on the operating table? I left the hospital and sought second and third opinions.

By the grace of heaven, the second and third cardiologists agreed with each other. "Deirdre, you have a small hole in your heart, but it is not significant enough to be causing these problems. Your condition is caused by a short circuit in the nerve impulses from your brain to your heart. You don't need surgery. You need to slow down. The trigger is too much stress."

I, a young high-tech professional, was being told to slow down? *Seriously? But I couldn't deny what my ticker was shouting loud and clear: It was time to wise up. I resumed my fast-paced, perpetual-progress lifestyle and tried to figure out what to do.*

If you are constantly or frequently in Tasmanian-devil mode, I hope that the exercises in Step 1: Put "Enjoy Life" Back on the Agenda will help you take a critical look at your to-do list without needing a medical scare or other unexpected event to motivate you. But wake-up calls to pay attention to what matters most to you can happen at any time and come from any direction:

- For Jackie, a flight attendant for United Airlines, it happened in the first few weeks after September 11, 2001—an incredibly frightful time to be on board an airplane. She called me with a desire to reevaluate her life and design a future in which she would use her natural talents, help others and live more spiritually.

- For John, a busy executive nearing retirement age, it was when two recently retired friends passed away within a short time. The losses shook him to the core and gave him a new view of his mortality. He asked me to help him find a way to make more time for the people he loved and take better care of his own health.

When you are distracted by a busy lifestyle, it is difficult to question your mental agenda on your own. So if you haven't had a wake-up call already, let this book be your wake-up call. As your personal life coach, I am telling you: If you want to change your life, you need to start by slowing down. Complete Exercise 6: Identify Your Wake-Up Call to determine what motivates you and remind yourself exactly why you have decided to dramatically change your life with the YOLO program.

EXERCISE 6:

Identify Your Wake-Up Call

What signal or event would force you to give serious thought to your life's direction and priorities? Has it happened to you already?

→ In your YOLO journal, jot down a few reasons why now is the time for you to change your life. Some questions to ask yourself are:

1. **What made me buy this book?**
2. **Why do I feel a pressing need to change my life right now?**
3. **What would I change about my life if I became seriously ill?**

The Benefits

Because busy-ness is pandemic in society, experts are constantly telling people to slow down and reevaluate their lifestyles. There are lots of reasons to do just that: to be happier, reduce stress, improve health and reduce demands on the environment. Unfortunately, knowing these benefits and knowing *how* to obtain them are not the same thing. Fortunately, in the rest of this chapter you will learn specific techniques to help you break free of the perpetual progress mind-set and slow down when you feel like your life is too hectic.

Consider the additional positive effects that slowing down can have on your life:

- **Increased mental clarity.** Slowing down calms your mind, allowing you to look within to understand what you truly want, and then make good life choices.

- **Closer relationships.** Taking time to connect with—and be aware of—your thoughts relieves stress and brings quiet focus. When with family and friends, you'll be able to deeply connect with them, mentally as well as physically, without your thoughts being pulled in other directions.

- **More accomplishments.** Taking time out for your self-care is a smart personal and professional decision, not an indulgence. It increases your energy, vitality and resilience while others allow their batteries to run low and burn out. You get more done when you are well-rested, self-aware and centered. Most successful CEOs can attest to the benefit of this strategy.

- **Increased creativity and innovation.** The best, most creative thoughts come to you when you are relaxed. You can access your brilliance when you break free of frenzied thinking. (In Step 5: Build Your Self-Confidence, you will see the utility of creative thought.)

- **Consistent progress.** When you ignore the need to recharge, you end up exhausted and need more time to recover your normal energy levels than if you had taken regular breaks along the way. By stopping the roller coaster of high- and low-energy extremes, you can keep moving steadily toward your goals.

- **Gain time.** When you break out of to-do thinking and take a moment to lift your head, take a deep breath and look around, those few minutes last much longer. (Consider how enjoyable—and enduring—three minutes feels when you're sitting outside in the sun, compared with three minutes when you're rushing around getting ready for work.)

All of these benefits will be invaluable to you as you work your way through the YOLO program to create dramatic change in your life.

Of course, slowing down takes discipline—I know. Chronic multitasking and overdoing can be deep-seated habits. After my diagnosis from the cardiologist, I initially found it difficult to slow down and listen to my own thoughts. The practice of being unhurried—living with focus instead of frenzy—is ongoing, not a one-time achievement. It may seem counterintuitive to do less in order to live more, but I learned that **doing more does not necessarily translate into living better.** I came to appreciate that there is much value in slowness and, most important, that slowing down is essential for making dramatic changes in your life.

Although many people equate the word *dramatic* with quick and hurried, it can also mean slow and evolving. Consider the unfolding of a great movie or play—often the plot builds slowly to a dramatic climax. Cultivating this kind of slow, deliberate pace is a discipline and life-long practice. Some days will be easier than others.

The first step in the shift toward a less frenzied lifestyle is to reject the allure of multitasking and begin monotasking: doing one task at a time. Monotasking involves resisting the temptation to pick up the phone while driving, clear the kitchen counter while drinking your morning coffee or answer email while on a phone call. Try it! Because you probably have become so accustomed to a busy lifestyle, it will not be easy to give up the habit.

To start this slowing-down process, complete Exercise 7: Start to Monotask. It may feel strange at first, but believe me, you can change your habits, and the benefits are well worth the effort!

> *Pat, a forty-year-old client who was working on transitioning from the corporate world to an artistic career told me, "Not only do living in the moment and noticing the good that surrounds you go hand in hand and inspire each other, they also add time to your life. I became more focused, stopped*

multitasking, did more things right the first time and had more energy all day. If I was feeling tired, I stopped and looked around. I noticed. And then I moved on, invigorated by what I saw and how lucky I was to see it."

EXERCISE 7:

Start to Monotask

By becoming a regular monotasker, you will create a solid base from which to begin the dramatic redesign of your future.

→ Choose any normal task (e.g., preparing food, eating a meal, checking email, talking on the phone or driving a car) and approach it with focus and singular attention. Limit yourself to that one task—don't allow yourself to be distracted. Notice how you first feel anxious about not getting enough done but soon begin to relax and enjoy the simplicity of this exercise.

Monotasking can be particularly relaxing when it comes to eating. At some point when you are home alone, sit down at a table with your snack or meal, and eat mindfully without reading the newspaper, flipping through the mail or watching TV.

Time to Smell the Roses

A peaceful mind generates power.

–Norman Vincent Peale

As you work through the YOLO program, you will learn to make happiness an integral part of your everyday existence. You will realize immediate benefit from each incremental choice, because prioritizing small activities you enjoy will make you happy—and that happiness then will spill over into the rest of your life. The resulting sense of increased control over your level of life satisfaction is a crucial foundation for making dramatic changes later.

In Exercise 7: Start to Monotask, you practiced doing one thing at a time. Next, you will learn additional slowing-down techniques for finding happiness in isolated, rejuvenating moments of each day.

Use this short poem as a reminder of the importance of slowing down. Keep it someplace where you will see it every day—on your desk, refrigerator or dashboard. I don't know who wrote it or what it's called; I call it "Slow Me Down."

Slow Me Down

Slow me down, ease my hurried pace;

Help me find true peace in a warm and gentle place.

Calm my worries, lift my fears, let my soul take rest;

Help me see the simple gifts that leave my life so blessed.

Break Time with a Purpose

Each day, be sure to take a momentary break from your efforts to enjoy one or more aspects of your current situation, whatever and wherever it may be. In this moment—which may last one minute or several—you will:

- Stop exerting yourself physically.
- Pause your mental agenda so you don't think about tasks not yet done.
- Simply appreciate your life.

I call this activity *coasting.* When you coast, you slow down and disengage your mind from the need to achieve. Your brain is refreshed and your energy level restored. At any time—especially when you're feeling overly rushed or catch yourself multitasking in a stressful way—ask yourself, "If I were to slow down for a minute, what could I enjoy about this moment?" Before you know it, you'll be back in touch with what makes you happy and slowly moving toward the life you want, one coasting moment at a time.

The term *coasting* came to me as I recalled riding my bicycle as a child. I would pedal hard to get to the top of a hill and then take my feet off of the pedals and just go, freewheeling down the other side. The air on my face and the feeling of flying were such a rush! I coasted as far as I could before pedaling again. Those effortless moments were pure, simple, easily attainable joy. And you can experience moments like that anytime you want.

When you let yourself coast, your awareness of the moment helps you to not only *appreciate* the experience but also *remember* it, thereby teaching you how to repeat the experience. I found this to be true one sunny day while I was finishing up my master's thesis in Dublin, Ireland—a place where cloudy weather prevails.

> *I sat outside the library with my friend and fellow student William, enjoying a rare moment of sunshine. "In the scheme of our lives," I mused out loud, "we are spending an insignificant few minutes here on this bench. But don't you think that short, pleasant, in-between times like this one, when added together, make up the overall feeling of joy in life? And isn't it a pity that we aren't likely to even remember these few minutes of sitting in the sun together ten or twenty years from now?"*

William feigned being insulted by the idea that I would not remember the conversation with him, but of course understood what I meant. The truth is, taking an impromptu study break with a friend—especially in the warmth of the rare

Dublin sun—was in no way insignificant; it is an example of coasting. Because I appreciated that moment and consciously made note of it (in this case, not only to myself but also to William), I've never forgotten it.

> *A client, Jaime, a business leader, recently described the search for everyday happiness as "about so much more than just a few happy moments. When I first started to do it, I assumed I would only feel pockets of happiness as I engaged in those activities I enjoyed. I found the effect to be much more far-reaching than that."*

To help you recall when you may have been coasting in the past, complete Exercise 8: Recall a Coasting Memory. By looking back at past coasting experiences, you can learn to identify and create them in the future.

EXERCISE 8:
Recall a Coasting Memory

Guess what? When you feel relaxed and at peace, happy and fully appreciative for just a moment, you are coasting—even if you don't know it!

→ Recall one experience when you took a break from whatever you were busy with to simply enjoy the moment. In your YOLO journal, list the elements that made the moment special for you. Some questions you might ask yourself include:

1. **What are the basic details? Where am I? Who am I with? What was I doing? How was I feeling?**
2. **What made me aware of my feelings in the moment?**
3. **Was this feeling triggered by an emotion, activity, sight or sound?**

Enjoy the happy feelings that accompany this recollection. Repeat this exercise with another memory, if you wish. You are now familiar with at least one way of coasting that works for you.

How to Coast

Remember, to coast, simply stop whatever you are doing, then find and appreciate whatever small joy is available to you in that moment. The beauty of coasting is that it can be done as a break from any task, even the most mundane!

For instance, while mopping the kitchen floor, you might normally be thinking about picking up the living room next. But instead, switch your mind-set to your immediate situation and surroundings: the feel of the floor beneath your feet and the mop in your hand, the sounds you hear, the sunlight you see coming through the window and the scent of the cleaning solution. A lemony scent may lead your mind to wander to memories of drinking fresh lemonade or your childhood home. Or perhaps the glistening floor will prompt a feeling of satisfaction in a job nearly done.

As in the mopping example, **coasting is often associated with a sensory experience—sight, sound, taste, touch or smell.** It also can be related to feelings that are evoked, such as love, pride, joy or gratitude. It may sound silly, but believe me, when you switch your focus from anxiety (e.g., finishing a task so you can get to the next one on your list) to a happy memory, a pleasurable sensory experience or a reward, you release your brain from the pressure of making perpetual progress and give your mental agenda a time-out. You restore your equilibrium and regain control of your time and priorities. Even though you will continue mopping at some point, your brain has been switched to a new, more relaxed state because you have recognized something good about your task, your day and your life.

This change of focus naturally lifts your spirits, shifting your mental environment from negative (anxieties, worries and concerns) to positive (possibilities, appreciation and gratitude). My clients report that in moments of coasting they experience feelings of creativity, well-being and plenty. They feel fully alive and recognize that in that instant they are reconnected to what makes them happy. Perhaps most important is their *awareness* of feeling relaxed and happy in the given situation.

To create dramatic change in your life, you must enjoy and create more coasting experiences, ultimately making them an essential ingredient of your days. For those who are life-long experts at making perpetual progress (sometimes called overachievers), coasting is a novel skill. Exercise 9: Learn to Coast: A Primer will help you become reacquainted with the feeling of coasting. Give coasting a try, and become familiar with more elements that create coasting moments for you. Together, let's all learn to become slower achievers!

EXERCISE 9:

Learn to Coast: A Primer

In Exercise 8: Recall a Coasting Memory, you reminded yourself what coasting feels like. Not sure how to make it happen in the present? No problem. You can start out slowly. Once you get the hang of it, you will begin to coast on your own.

→ Take a brief (one- to three-minute) pause from your work on the YOLO program to do anything that engages another sense or allows you to appreciate life and feel happy. For example:

- **Listen to music, draw a picture, savor a treat or smell a flower.**
- **List the ten people who mean the most to you in the world.**
- **Identify as many items of beauty as you can see from where you are right now.**

If you feel a bit awkward or anxious while coasting, don't worry; it will start to feel more natural with practice. More important, do you feel refreshed and reenergized afterward?

→ Next, try to work coasting into each day until it becomes a habit. Any of the following situations are particularly good opportunities for coasting:

- **Waiting (for a meeting to start, in traffic or in a line)**
- **Working on a tedious project at home or at work**
- **Doing a routine errand or task (such as grocery shopping or making photocopies)**
- **Feeling frazzled by any situation**

Whenever you need to remind yourself how and when to coast, repeat this mantra: "When frazzled, dazzle!" Look around for anything that dazzles you, physically or mentally. Do you see something colorful or interesting? Does an aroma or sound evoke a pleasant memory? Did you just do something really well? Enjoy that moment!

When and Where to Coast

Coasting can be experienced in three ways. *Spontaneous coasting* is an unexpected moment of happiness that pleasantly surprises you without your needing to make it happen; for example, you might think to yourself, "This is as perfect as this moment could ever be" or "I feel so lucky right now." You may need to consciously train yourself to notice and take advantage of coasting opportunities when they arise; be on the lookout for innumerable *opportunistic coasting* moments. Finally, in situations when you need a break, you might need to create *deliberate coasting* moments.

I explain these three approaches to coasting next.

Spontaneous Coasting

When a wonderful coasting moment happens on its own, unexpectedly, all you need to do is recognize and appreciate it to enjoy and remember the happy feelings it evokes.

You might have experienced a moment like this one before:

> *You are inside, working intently on a project when you suddenly notice that it has started to rain. The falling rain pulls your attention toward the window for a moment. You watch, marveling at the force with which it falls. With your work on hold, you are no longer thinking about your next task. As you are captivated by and appreciating the nature right outside, you are coasting.*

A coasting moment becomes more valuable when you *notice* that it is a coasting moment. Conscious recognition of the break allows you to feel it more deeply and be grateful for it. Also, by noticing that you are coasting, you will learn which kinds of situations help you pause and enjoy life.

When was the last time you let yourself get lost in a pleasant distraction? Complete Exercise 10: Open Up to Spontaneous Coasting to identify such a moment and learn how to enjoy such happy moments more often.

EXERCISE 10:

Open Up to Spontaneous Coasting

In Exercise 9: Learn to Coast: A Primer, you started working toward a daily coasting practice. One way to become more aware of spontaneous coasting is to record the moments after they occur.

→ Over the next few days, keep your YOLO journal close at hand and list any spontaneous coasting moments that come your way. Write down where you were, what was happening, who you were with and any other details that seem pertinent.

Some questions you might ask yourself about that moment are:

1. What made it so wonderful?
2. How did I feel? Lucky? Cherished? Talented? Free?
3. What made me feel this way?
4. What was I grateful for?

Paying attention to these enjoyable moments gives them importance, and giving importance to them brings greater happiness to your life. Keep coasting to continue toward the life you want.

Opportunistic Coasting

To live the life you truly love, it is essential to recognize and take full advantage of opportunistic coasting moments that may present themselves in your daily life. Don't let a potential moment of happiness slip away!

Here's an example from a morning when I was busily preparing for a business trip via commuter bus to Boston, about an hour and fifteen minutes from my home in Maine.

> *I was going over my work agenda for the day when my eye was drawn to the outside: wispy white clouds across a vivid blue sky; the silver glint of a jet, leaving behind its trace as two streams of ethereal white vapor; lush green trees reaching into the sky. The vibrant mix of colors—white, blue, silver and green—looked like a photograph. I realized, "This is the most quiet, contemplative moment I'm likely to get all day. Even though I have a lot to work on, I'm going to purposefully coast for a few minutes and enjoy this spectacular sight."*
>
> *Still gazing out the window, I marveled at the view. The bright sunlight illuminated the edges of some clouds but not others; the branches of the trees were so full; the plane's trace faded away ever-so-slowly. The scene changed each moment, never to be exactly the same again.*

When I returned to my work, my stress level was lower and I was able to appreciate the good fortune of having pleasant weather for my business trip. By coasting, I was able to effortlessly and pleasantly shift my perspective from negative (stress that I had been feeling about my obligations) to positive (gratitude for my current situation). Had I not chosen to coast for those few minutes, I probably would have spent the entire trip worrying and arrived like a wound-up top ready to spin out of control. Instead, I enjoyed several relaxing moments of beauty and was able to continue my day in a better, more calm frame of mind.

Opportunities for coasting present themselves every day. The trick is to recognize and take advantage of them. Here are some potential situations in which coasting moments might arise:

- When passing by a window, look outside and notice the sunlight reflecting off of other buildings and structures.
- While doing household chores, let your kids convince you to join in an impromptu game of hide-and-seek or tag.
- When outdoors, listen to the chirping of the songbirds, admire the spectrum of colors in the garden or feel the breeze on your open palms.
- When preparing a cup of tea or coffee, pour in the cream and watch it swirl artistically as it mixes in and take a deep whiff of the aroma before the first sip.

If none of these opportunities sounds like something you'd enjoy, don't fret—each person appreciates different things, and your coasting moments will be uniquely personal. One person might coast while enjoying a moment of freedom between meetings; another might coast while eating, marveling at the flavors of a dish.

Coasting moments can be found everywhere. Complete Exercise 11: Identify Opportunities for Coasting to learn how to notice and take advantage of yours.

EXERCISE 11:

Identify Opportunities for Coasting

Review the coasting moments that you recorded in your YOLO journal for Exercise 8: Recall a Coasting Memory, Exercise 9: Learn to Coast: A Primer, and Exercise 10: Open Up to Spontaneous Coasting.

→ In another entry in your YOLO journal, jot down the aspects of coasting that were common among your coasting experiences. To guide this exercise, ask yourself,

1. What kinds of situations allowed me to coast in the past?
2. Did I particularly enjoy any of the model coasting situations in Exercise 9: Learn to Coast: A Primer? Why did I relate to some more than others?
3. What are the common elements of my favorite spontaneous coasting moments? Are they sensory (sight, hearing, touch, taste or smell)? Emotional? Both?
4. What trends are apparent from my favorite ways to coast?

Armed with this list characterizing situations or environments that allow you to coast, you'll begin to recognize opportunities to take advantage of these rejuvenating moments.

Deliberate Coasting

Moments of coasting become even more frequent when you start to consciously create them. A consistent practice of deliberate coasting will keep your mind fresh, creative and in tune with what makes you happy.

One of my favorite deliberate coasting moments follows:

> *Shortly after moving to Maine, I woke up early one day in June and stepped onto the porch to get the newspaper. What a beautiful day greeted me! I decided to go for a power walk on the local beach.*
>
> *The tide was high and the morning fog was still hanging over the sea. The scene was quintessential Maine: Two lobster boats floated just offshore, and a foghorn bellowed in the distance. Instead of continuing with my plan to get sweaty by marching mechanically up and down the beach with mental blinders on, I deliberately chose to change my plan and acquiesce to my surroundings. The beauty of the scene inspired me to slow down; drink in the sights, sounds and smells; breathe deeply; and enjoy the moment.*
>
> *And so I sat. I watched. I breathed. I listened. I contemplated. The experience was magical, and nothing could have improved it. Instead of ticking items off my mental agenda, I felt grateful to be living in Maine and having the time and opportunity to enjoy such a peaceful morning. There would be plenty of time for power walking later.*

If I hadn't deliberately changed plans and created this moment of coasting, I would've missed out on a powerful opportunity to do something that set a relaxed, resourceful tone for the rest of my day.

Below are some interesting ways in which my clients have created deliberate coasting moments in their lives. Some of these ideas might be old hat to you; others might be brand new. Feel free to borrow from this list or create your own. These deliberate coasting ideas are listed in approximate order from shorter to longer in duration, under the assumption that as your coasting becomes a habit, you will coast for longer periods.

- Take four deep breaths. Pay attention to the physical sensations of your chest and abdomen expanding, and visualize the vital oxygen moving into your bloodstream.
- While washing your hands, enjoy the feeling of the hot soapy water on the insides of your wrists.
- Walking outdoors, feel the temperature of the air on your face and neck.
- For a few moments, quietly observe the world around you—people, flowers, birds and sky—whatever is happening, wherever you are.
- Instead of your usual five- or ten-minute shower, indulge in a twenty-minute bath instead. The calming powers of submersion may surprise you!
- Drive in the slow lane, in silence.
- Relax in your favorite chair and read a novel for thirty minutes, relishing the cozy feeling of home.
- Attend a one-hour yoga or tai chi class and slowly stretch mind and limbs to their full potential.
- On a warm night, go outside, lie down and gaze up at the cosmos. Stay there until you see a satellite, a shooting star or both.
- Plan a relaxed weekend of cooking time to indulge your sense of culinary adventure and feelings of abundance.

Has this list sparked some ideas for you? Sometimes coasting is solitary, in connection with oneself; other times it involves interaction with others. My husband is a musician, and he often refers to the happiness he experiences when playing music in sync with others. In contrast, some people delight in the peacefulness of walking a mountain trail alone, appreciating the natural world. Most people do some coasting alone and some with others.

A deliberate coasting moment suits *your* preferences, lifestyle and perspective. It might mean taking a minute to listen to the end of a song on the car radio after you have reached your destination, lingering to enjoy the smell of baking bread as you pass a bakery or sitting on a park bench to savor a treat before returning to your office after lunch. Even in the busiest metropolis, you can notice a flower blooming through a crack in the sidewalk or appreciate the myriad colors in the fashions of passersby.

Complete Exercise 12: Create Deliberate Coasting Moments and learn how to give yourself a well-deserved break whenever you need it.

EXERCISE 12:
Create Deliberate Coasting Moments

Here's a special two-part challenge:

→ Make a point of creating at least one short (one- to three-minute) deliberate coasting moment per day, from now until you finish this book. Some planning questions to consider are:

1. **When will I take the time to plan and schedule these moments—perhaps Sunday evening for the week ahead, or as I start each day before breakfast?**

2. When is the best time of day for me to take my coasting breaks—in other words, when do I feel most frazzled?

3. What sort of coasting works well for me—spending a few minutes sitting or walking alone? Will I vary it from day to day or keep the same routine each day?

4. How long do I need to coast each time to feel rejuvenated? Do I need to make any special arrangements (e.g., adjusting a work schedule, scheduling babysitting duties) to take this time for myself?

5. Will I need a reminder to take my daily coasting moment? If so, what sort of reminder works best for me? An auditory alarm? A digital message? A written note?

→ At the end of the first week, schedule a five-minute coasting check-in with yourself. About your planned coasting time, ask yourself,

6. Did I tensely watch the clock, or could I find something to enjoy about each moment?

7. Did the time seem to go by quickly or slowly?

8. Did I have any insights about my day or my life?

Record your observations about deliberate coasting moments in your YOLO journal.

Helpful Hints

As you work through the steps in this book, I invite you to **slow the pace of your daily life and continue to create moments of coasting whenever and wherever you can.** Once you learn to savor these opportunities, the benefits will become clear.

When you begin this practice, you may hear discouraging internal voices that try to sabotage your efforts to coast: "This is unrealistic, you don't have time for this!" or "You can't slow down and still get everything done!" Negative beliefs related to years of exposure to the perpetual progress mind-set may chime in with age-old sayings like, "Life isn't that simple" and "You have to keep your nose to the grindstone."

> *Kelly was a bored and burned-out project manager working for a major pharmaceutical company in New York when she sought my services. Because she wanted to add some kind of artfulness to her life, her first effort to slow down and develop a regular coasting practice was to notice "something beautiful" every day. At first she sometimes forgot until bedtime, but over time she began to recognize that "beauty is all around—I just needed to open my eyes and notice it."*

> *The process was difficult at first. "Whenever I started to have these anxious thoughts, I used them as a cue to call myself back to the present," she says. "If I remembered to be present, I noticed what was happening around me and all sorts of beautiful things."*

> *Today Kelly is a cheerful, vibrant artist and writer fulfilling her dream of living in Istanbul, Turkey.*

Remind yourself that if you never slow down, you won't have the chance to find the answers to important questions—like, "What will make my life happier?" Also remember that many people before you have successfully slowed down and now live new lives they love.

You must slow down to be able to create your ideal life, no matter how loud your subconscious protests. Trust your resolve; you can do this! If you need support, ask a friend for reassurance or seek out a life coach or a counselor to help you get past the difficult messages.

Repeat the mantra: "When frazzled, dazzle!"

Not only are the rewards of coasting immediately gratifying, but the remaining four steps for dramatically redesigning your future *depend* on being able to coast, particularly Step 2: Go Inward to Find Your Answers. Read on to find out how!

STEP TWO

Go Inward to Find Your Answers

To move toward a life that you will love, you must consult the greatest source of wisdom available: your own. Learn to connect with your truest, deepest desires, then leverage that truth by choosing words and actions that improve your life.

All progress begins by asking a better question.

~Robert Stuberg

Terms Used in This Chapter

inner sage: an innate source of important life answers; the voice of one's absolute truth, understanding and insight

self-knowledge: the state of being readily connected to one's own thoughts, ideas, emotions, preferences and desires

no-lie policy: the choice to speak only one's honest truth rather than fib, avoid or lie

Believe it or not, each person has within all the answers necessary for achieving their ideal life, but most people don't know how to access those answers within themselves. When someone is working with a real live life coach (instead of a book), the regular coaching calls or meetings are scheduled appointments that necessarily put daily life on hold, allowing the client to slow down for deep thought and introspection about important life questions.

In Step 2: Go Inward to Find Your Answers, you will learn the tools and techniques required to simulate that "live" coaching experience on your own. You, too, can access your own innate wisdom through quiet reflection.

Your Source of Truth

At the center of your being you have the answer; you know who you are and you know what you want.

~Lao-tzu

Hidden deep inside every person are the answers to all of their questions. Most people are familiar with the idea of an "inner child"—the one who wants to eat ice cream all day and hates when people tell them what to do! But they also possess a wise voice within that I call an inner sage. It is the source of these important answers and more, and learning to listen to your inner sage is another foundation step of the You Only Live Once (YOLO) program. Unfortunately, when in the tight grip of a perpetual progress mind-set and focused on a mental agenda, people tend to flounder, full of questions but unable to hear the answers.

You may think that it's simplistic to consider that each person has all the answers within, but this knowledge is profound. **If you learn to listen to your innate wisdom, you can make informed choices about your life.**

Your inner sage represents your deepest wisdom, most thoughtful judgment and most useful experience. It can guide you in a way similar to helpful advice that might be offered by a grandparent, respected leader or trusted elder. Your inner sage is more than just gut instinct; it is the voice of your absolute truth, understanding and insight.

How do I know that you have an inner sage? Because every single person I have worked with has been able to tune in to this authentic voice after learning how. As a result, they were able to gain perspective, break through barriers of fear and create a clear path to happiness.

Inner Sage

People may refer to their inner sage as the voice of the smartest person they know, a best friend or simply their highest and best self. How you conceptualize it does not matter; what does matter is learning to listen to it consistently.

Some people never ask themselves hard questions until they are faced with a wake-up call—usually in the form of a serious life event—that changes their perspective. In my case, heart palpitations caused me to question the validity of my perpetual progress mind-set (see Step 1: Put "Enjoy Life" Back on the Agenda) and learn to slow down. Then, a challenging conversation at work pushed me to look inward for the answers I needed about my life.

> *The software company I worked for was bought out, and a chaotic transition ensued. As a manager, I was relieved when the executives brought in consultant and executive coach Mike Whitehead to help us get the company back on track. His insightful feedback kept us focused and effective.*
>
> *At the end of one exhaustingly long day, Mike popped his head into my office. "You seem stressed out tonight," he said, never one to mince words. "What's up?"*

I distractedly replied, "Nothing out of the ordinary." He then asked more directly, "What do you want?" My automatic reply was that I wanted the database to work, the sales guys to get the purchase orders right and collections to get off my back.

Laughing, Mike cut to the chase: "Deirdre, in the big scheme of things, do you want to be working here in five years?" That question got my attention. Why was he asking me this? Had my boss asked him to?

In truth, the job that I had loved no longer existed. Most of my favorite colleagues were gone, and I missed their camaraderie, teamwork and friendship. What's more, with the recent changes, days had gotten longer and more stressful. I recalled my cardiologist's instruction to slow down and, deep down, knew that my answer to Mike should be no. Instead I hedged: "I haven't thought about it, but I suppose not."

"Well," Mike responded, "I had a feeling change was in the air for you." He also clarified that his comments were personal, not from higher-ups. Then, seemingly out of nowhere, he asked, "What do you want from your life?"

I thought for a minute before answering tentatively, "I guess I want to work with great colleagues and positive energy." Then I began to pick up steam. "I also want a family and more balance in my life, and I want to help other people have balance, too. I want to be focused on people's happiness." The truth I knew inside myself came tumbling out, loud and clear.

Mike smiled, in an amused and knowing way, and asked, "So, what's next?" When I admitted that I didn't know, he asked, "Have you thought about coaching?"

Mike's inquiry urged me to think about the next phases of my life and career; his questions unearthed a new consciousness about my desires. I began to look inside myself and found that hidden beneath my perpetual progress mind-set was a people-centered person who wanted to live a more meaningful life.

Even though it is the best authority on your happiness, your inner sage is quiet and calls for your focused, undivided attention. Complete Exercise 13: Meet Your Inner Sage to become acquainted with this voice of wisdom within.

EXERCISE 13:

Meet Your Inner Sage

Go to www.YouOnlyLiveOnceBook.com/readergift and download your free copy of this exercise so that you can fully relax and experience a true meeting with your Inner Sage.

Find someplace quiet where you can be alone and uninterrupted for about fifteen minutes.

→ Coast for a minute or two to quiet your body and mind in preparation for this exercise.

1. **Sit comfortably and take a few relaxing, deep breaths. Rest your hands on your lap or clasp them loosely together, whichever feels more natural. Close your eyes.**

Notes: At this point, your mind may give you a physical inventory (e.g., "Feet are cold" or "Back is achy"). Don't ignore these messages; instead, acknowledge them (e.g., respond, "I'll get to you in a minute [cold feet or achy back]; right now I'm seeking an answer to a question"). If you hear negative backtalk (e.g., "This doesn't work" or "I don't have time for this"), acknowledge and respond to those messages, too (e.g., "I am just experimenting and giving something new a try—no promises, no commitments"); if you don't, they will block access to your inner sage.

2. Next, take a deep breath and ask yourself something that has been on your mind today—perhaps a decision, big or small, that you have been trying to make.

3. Wait a few minutes to give your inner sage time to respond. Just sit calmly, relax and listen. You will know that you are hearing the wisdom of your inner sage when the answer feels completely true and honest, as if you had known it all along. (In fact, you have!) Immediately, you will feel a wave of relief from finding the answer to your question. You may even feel the desire to take immediate action based on your new clarity.

Note: This exercise is particularly difficult to do when you are feeling troubled or anxious. If you have a hard time reaching your inner sage, you may need to slow down more before you begin; your mind may be too busy worrying to be able to relax and allow access to your inner wisdom. For now, take a break and try again later. When you're ready, go back to your notes from Step 1: Put "Enjoy Life" Back on the Agenda, pick one of your favorite coasting methods and do it. Then try this exercise again from the first step.

How and When to Listen

The busier people get, the less time they take for themselves—even though they need it *more.* When things get busy, there's no time to coast. Ironically, the less you coast, the weaker the voice of your inner sage—in other words, when you most desperately need to listen to your innate wisdom, you cannot hear it.

Coasting, which you learned to do in Step 1: Put "Enjoy Life" Back on the Agenda, helps you avoid mental exhaustion by enjoying slow moments between busy ones. Equally important, coasting turns up the volume on your inner sage. So as you continue your coasting practice, tune in and listen. The things you hear will amaze you!

The Big Picture

One way to practice hearing the wisdom of your inner sage is to explore what you want in the bigger scheme of things. A great way to do this is to ponder what you want your legacy to be. I often ask new clients how their inner sage wants them to be remembered, and here are some of the typical answers:

- Considerate, kind and thoughtful person
- Good parent
- Person who took time to be with friends and family
- Hard worker
- Someone who made a contribution to society, especially to those less fortunate
- Good daughter or son
- Person who lived life to the fullest, had no regrets and left something to inspire others

In most cases, acknowledging these desires clarifies the disconnect that people feel between what they want to be and how they are currently living their lives. In other words, what they are doing will not leave behind the legacy they intend.

A few months after my insightful discussion with Mike (and while still working at the same company), I took a business trip to Europe. In the airplane, halfway across the Atlantic Ocean, my laptop computer's battery died. I was forced to abandon my planned agenda. With nowhere to go and no work to do, I started coasting—staring out the window. Soon after, I took a pen and a pad of sticky notes out of my briefcase and started scribbling. What appeared on the little yellow squares came straight from my inner sage. In miniscule chicken scratchings, I effectively wrote my own funeral eulogy.

Although I cannot tell you why those words came out of me at that moment, I clearly recall what they were. Here is some of what my inner sage said to me that day:

> *I want to be remembered for recognizing the importance of putting relationships first. I want to be thought of as someone who strove to be a good wife, parent, friend, daughter, sister, co-worker and any other one-on-one role I might take on. I want to be remembered for caring, listening, supporting and believing in the people who grace my lifetime. I want to be remembered for being considerate and kind and for making a difference to others in some way.*

During that cramped seven-hour flight, I learned what my life was about. It wasn't any specific career, material possessions or to-do list item; it was about giving away what I felt was the best of me. It was about serving others from my heart, no matter where I was or what I was doing. When I slowed down, my inner sage was able to break through and be heard.

For me, caring for others was an important element of loving my life, and this desire wasn't reaching its full potential in my career at the time. After that memorable "talk" with my inner sage, I finally began investigating careers that felt more appropriate, like counseling and life coaching.

What has your inner sage been telling (or wanting to tell) you? Complete Exercise 14: Flash Forward to Discover What Really Matters for some insights.

EXERCISE 14:

Flash Forward to Discover What Really Matters

A common exercise for helping people discover what really matters is writing their own eulogy. Even though the concept may seem a bit strange, I believe that the process is an effective way to connect with your inner sage.

→ Imagine that you have only a few hours to live. You are lying in a comfortable bed with warm sunlight on your face. You are reflecting on your life with quiet contentment.

Ask yourself the following questions, and write the answers in your YOLO journal:

1. Before the end comes, who do I wish to see? (These people are most important to you.)

2. If I could be young again for a day, what would I wish to do? (You should do these favorite activities more frequently.)

3. Looking back without the impediment of modesty, what would I honestly say were the things I was naturally good at? (You should use these talents more often.)

Finally, in your YOLO journal, write the answers to the following questions, in as many words as it takes:

4. Who is in attendance at my funeral?

5. Who is (or are) giving my eulogy?

6. What is being said about me—how am I remembered by my family, friends, neighbors, co-workers and acquaintances?

Let your answers to these questions help you choose how to live your life and how to create the legacy that you hope to leave behind.

Strategic Questions

Thinking about what you want requires learning to regularly listen to your inner sage. Your ideal life becomes much easier to create when the questions are answered ahead of time. It's like planning a route before embarking on a road trip; you will be far less likely to make wrong turns, waste time or get lost along the way.

The next level of the YOLO program is finding answers to strategic questions that will help you create this new life you want. Luckily for you, your inner sage does more than just talk. It listens, and it responds to inquiry!

I first consulted my inner sage at a workshop with life coach Cheryl Richardson in Boston, one day before I was to start a new high-tech position. With Cheryl's guidance, I strategically accessed my inner sage "on demand." I asked my inner sage to show me three issues that needed attention, and it gave me the necessary answers: Work was running my life, my health required more attention and I missed spending time with the people who were important to me. I left that workshop inspired and invigorated; my values and priorities were clear. Since that day, I have taken thousands of small steps toward fulfilling the needs that my inner sage identified that day: I work less, take better care of my health and spend lots of time with family and close friends. And I enjoy my life so much more as a result.

This technique of using your inner sage as a strategic resource is particularly relevant for a person who is unhappy in a job or career. With new career-change clients, I always start by helping them become acquainted with their inner sage because it helps them identify an ideal career infinitely more quickly and successfully. For these clients, slowing down, breathing deeply and asking their inner sage about their work life is an empowering experience. They often are stunned to find immediate answers to questions they've spent months or even years researching in books, seminars and classes. The most important information—what kind of career would be deeply fulfilling—was within them the whole time.

> *A young software engineer named Kate called me and said, "I am stuck. I have no idea where I am going with my life. My outlook is pretty bleak. I feel like I have woken up and found myself living a life I don't want."*
>
> *I guided Kate to coast and tune in to her inner sage, then asked her about her earlier goals and dreams. She got excited when she started talking about a biomedical engineering class that she had taken in college. She had loved working to understand how heart attacks occur. After ten years of working with computers, she didn't think it was possible to get back into the biology field; however, a little research revealed that she had applicable computer skills to apply for a position with a company developing an artificial heart for critically ill patients.*
>
> *After starting her new position, Kate wrote to me, "This process broke me out of my old habits and made me grow. I have learned so much about myself. I feel like I have rediscovered the passion that I had when I knew where I wanted my life to go."*
>
> *Essentially, Kate needed an opportunity to slow down and connect with her inner sage. When she did, her authentic desires were easily heard. Imagine if she had never learned to listen to, believe in and trust her inner sage!*

Complete Exercise 15: Consult Your Inner Sage—the exercise that Cheryl Richardson led during the workshop. You will learn to query your inner sage on demand and gain valuable answers.

EXERCISE 15:
Consult Your Inner Sage

As in Exercise 13: Meet Your Inner Sage, begin by sitting comfortably and taking a few relaxing, deep breaths.

→ Place your hands in your lap or clasp them loosely together—whichever feels more natural to you—and close your eyes. Remember that at first your mind may give you a physical inventory (e.g., "My shoes are too tight" or "This chair is hard"). Just breathe deeply and acknowledge these messages (e.g., respond, "I'll get to you in a minute [tight shoes or hard chair]; right now I'm seeking an answer to a question").

Next, ask your inner sage to help you identify three issues in your life that need attention. Sit comfortably, keep breathing and notice what comes up.

After a few minutes, open your eyes and write the three issues in your YOLO journal. (Make sure that they're clearly marked and easy to find, because you'll revisit these issues in Step 3: Design Your Ideal Life).

If You Resist …

Did you find yourself avoiding the last three exercises for no obvious reason? Do you believe that you don't have an inner sage? Have you resisted tapping in to your true thoughts because you're afraid of what you might discover? Don't worry; you are not alone, and you can overcome these barriers (and others) to achieving the life you want. Fear does not need to hold you back.

For many people, the roots of resistance to *self-knowledge*—a ready connection to one's own thoughts, ideas, emotions, preferences and desires—are the same kinds of fears: of change, the unknown, success, failure or the truth. People don't want to discover things they don't like. To protect themselves from these scary options, they dismiss inner contemplation as a waste of time, something needed only by people with "issues," in psychotherapy or on television talk shows.

To live a life you love, you must expose and address these fears—with a friend, a coach, a partner or a professional counselor—so you can start regularly using this powerful resource within yourself. I had to address my fears before I was able to take the first steps toward my present life.

> *When contemplating Mike's career suggestion and my own discoveries about what I really wanted, I realized that I was afraid to leave my job. I wasn't afraid of losing income—although that idea was certainly scary—but of being aimless. The thought of having no idea about where, when or how I would move forward in life was petrifying. If I was no longer an up-and-coming leader in the high-tech industry, who the heck was I? Almost as if running across rocks in a stream, I was afraid that if I hesitated, I'd end up in the water.*
>
> *As a result, I stopped paying attention to my inner sage. I spent two more years in the same line of work, blinded by security, ego and the social legitimacy of rising through the ranks (ah, the perpetual progress mind-set!). I continued to look in the wrong place for life satisfaction, not unlike looking for eggs in an apple tree.*

Fear makes it difficult to hear your inner sage because many loud, nay-saying voices can drown out one soft, wise voice. To get past the fear and the resulting inertia, you must get to the source of that fear. Complete Exercise 16: Dissolve Your Fear to bring it out into the open and then challenge its validity.

EXERCISE 16:

Dissolve Your Fear

To move past your fear, you must first expose it to daylight. People often keep their fears private, where they can never be challenged. Once in the light, most fears dissolve quite readily.

Think about any fear that is holding you back. Ask someone you trust—your life coach, partner or a friend—to be your sounding board, in person or over the phone, not in email or texts. Speaking the fear aloud brings it into the realm of the ordinary—a situation like any other that needs to be considered, studied and resolved.

→ Find a quiet, uninterrupted time and place to get together. First, share your fear. Next, have the other person ask you the following questions, allowing you plenty of time to be silent, think and respond before continuing to the next question.

1. What is the worst thing that could happen if you tried to do what you're afraid of?
2. What would you do if [the answer to question #1] happened?
3. What do you stand to lose by trying [the answer to question #2]?
4. What might you gain by trying [the answer to question #2]?

Next, ask your partner to support you, in person or on the phone, in doing the activity that you were afraid of. For example, consider that you'd like some support for your first on-demand consultation with your inner sage. If you are comfortable consulting your inner sage in the presence of the other person, ask them to read the first three paragraphs of Exercise 13: Meet Your Inner Sage to you in a slow, soft voice and then give you time to sit in silent contemplation.

If you prefer, ask your partner to "bookend" with you. What this means is that they speak with you for a few minutes, then leave you alone. You do whatever you've been avoiding, on your own, while they wait. Then they plan to speak with you again for a few minutes immediately afterward. This approach will give you the comfort of knowing you have support before and after you face (and conquer) your fear.

How to Move Forward

Most people readily agree that there is great value in self-knowledge. Surprisingly, though, some of my most intelligent, successful clients shy away from it. Even though they may have felt overwhelmed (e.g., by job stress, relationship troubles or physical illness), they still resisted looking for answers within because they simply were afraid of the truth their inner sage might reveal. Instead, they remained caught up in the perpetual progress mind-set, running through their mental agendas day after day.

These people reached out for my help because their business-as-usual strategy wasn't working. They were unhappy and ready for change, yet they resisted slowing down and engaging in inward thoughts because *they didn't trust themselves* to be able to handle their own truth. They were afraid that looking within could lead to larger realizations about how off-course their lives had become, forcing them to confront the need for change before they were ready. It was the proverbial head-in-the-sand ostrich philosophy: If I don't see it, it's not really there! These clients needed the reassurance that ultimately they were in control of all decisions about their life, including when and whether to make changes.

While working on this book, I had a conversation about self-knowledge with Alan, a good friend from college. He's a smart, philosophical guy, and I asked him why he thought so few people consult their inner sage. He said, "I think we resist self-knowledge because it's very hard to understand the benefit when you only have limited glimpses of what it can do for you."

Alan's answer gave me new insight into how I could help people trust their own wisdom. Many people have experienced contact with their inner sage only sporadically, and maybe only a few times in their life—for instance, when going through rites of passage such as school graduation, first love or leaving home for the first time. They have not been taught to consult their inner sage except when in emotional upheaval. If this is the case, no wonder people don't want to turn to it regularly.

Try to think differently; getting to know your inner sage and consulting it on a regular basis can be your strategic advantage in life. It's not just a new age abstract concept. *Your inner sage is the best tool you have for connecting with your own convictions and, ultimately, experiencing more joy in your life.* As my father—always the talented handyman around the house—used to tell me, "Use the right tool for the right job. Using the right tool makes the job quicker and easier, and you get it done right the first time." Your inner sage is the right tool for the job—creating the life you want.

You must start consulting this wisdom all the time, whenever you need an answer to a question—that is, whenever you are procrastinating, hesitating, second-guessing yourself or feeling doubt. To do that, create regular quiet moments for your inner sage to speak to you, and be ready to listen! You will become an adept self-listener as you create your new future.

A Strong Connection

No legacy is so rich as honesty.

–William Shakespeare

Once a person recognizes the reliability of their inner sage and begins to consult it regularly, the practice gets easier and becomes a habit. The best way to strengthen this connection is to use it: Speak the truth aloud.

Unfortunately, many people have adopted the lazy habit of not telling the truth, typically to avoid potential conflict. They might say that they're sick to get out of engagements they don't want to attend, or claim that they're too busy to see people they don't want to spend time with. They also might lie to themselves, perpetuating such fibs as "I'm not overcommitted" and "I'll start exercising next week." They tell these little white lies because they have not yet developed the ability to be honest about their true desires. People lie because it's easier than being honest, but all lies are damaging and prevent them from facing reality, thus blocking them from taking action that supports their best interests.

Speaking the truth can be challenging, but it doesn't have to mean acting selfish, cruel or withdrawn. In fact, people who speak their truth can be more loving, generous and giving as a result. They protect their personal resources of energy, love and vitality while cherishing relationships and distributing their time wisely where and how they choose.

It is one thing to *think* about what you want; it is another to make it happen. Allow your deepest desires to move from wishing and hoping to action. **What your inner sage tells you is your absolute truth.** To speak your absolute truth, you must:

- Be acutely aware of your deepest wants and needs from your inner sage.
- Value your own happiness enough to choose to honor these wants and needs.

- Be willing to set clear boundaries with others regarding what you will and will not do, give or allow.
- Accept invitations that will expand your happiness and vitality.
- Decline requests that are not in your best interests.

Of course, putting these concepts into practice isn't always easy. For instance, imagine that a friend invites you to attend a charity benefit party. You don't want to attend but would feel guilty saying no. You are tempted to say yes—to be polite, avoid awkwardness, do the right thing, be a good person, or any other reasons that come to mind. You also know deep down that attending will make you feel miserable. In other words, saying yes would directly contradict your inner sage.

What do you do? First, resist the urge to answer immediately. Give yourself time to plan a response. Ask for permission to respond later. You might say something like, "Thanks for the invitation; it sounds like a good cause. Can I get back to you on it? When do you need to know?" (Let's imagine that she needs to know tomorrow.)

Next, find a time to slow down, reflect and consult your inner sage about this situation. Let's assume that your inner sage reminds you that you never enjoy these events and that when you force yourself to go, you end up regretting your decision. It cautions you that it has been a long week and notes honestly that you would prefer to stay home and watch TV. However, it also recognizes that you don't want to offend your friend or appear unsupportive because the event seems important to her and it is a worthwhile charity.

Taking all of this into account, plan your response. It might sound something like this: "Thanks for your invitation. I think it's an important cause and know you have put a lot of effort into it, so I want to support you and the charity. To be honest, though, I don't enjoy attending these types of events. Is there another way I can help?"

With an answer like this, you stay true to yourself, communicate a desire to help and show support for your friend and her cause while protecting yourself from an unwanted commitment. To take it a step further, you could have asked your inner sage what sort of help you would be willing to provide and offered that instead (e.g., "Can I make a donation?").

My client Emily had a hard time speaking her truth. While we were working together, she was employed by an agency that frequently sent her on out-of-town assignments.

> *Emily came to our coaching call feeling really angry and upset because her company had called that morning and asked her to leave that day on an assignment. She had planned to spend a quiet evening with her fiancé and was very disappointed. When I asked why she had agreed to go at the last minute, she admitted that she was afraid to say no.*
>
> *Emily remembered other situations in which she had given in to her employer's unreasonable demands over the years. Once, she was overseas on vacation with her parents when the company insisted that she return immediately for a project. She recalled being exhausted by the jet lag afterward: "I couldn't do anything. I just flopped down on the couch and slept for ten hours."*
>
> *Another time, the agency called with an assignment when Emily's fiancé's family was visiting and she had planned a special dinner. "The agency said, 'You are refusing an assignment because of dinner plans?' making it seem so trivial." Sadly, Emily gave in and canceled her dinner party.*

Emily felt that she had no power to say no to her agency. She wasn't lying to them but was lying to herself about her priorities and was afraid to act on her truth.

> *She told me her fear: "They will think badly of me and might not give me more work."*

Refusing an assignment could result in forfeiting future work; that threat was a reality. What Emily realized during our conversation was that lying to herself about what really mattered was taking a bigger toll in the long run; her happiness was being pushed aside in favor of someone else's demands. Emily needed to speak her truth to protect her life satisfaction.

Your True Voice

Don't ignore your truth! Agreeing to do something that you'll later regret is in direct opposition to your inner wisdom. If you do it anyway, you'll be disappointed with the circumstances and frustrated with yourself.

It's important to speak up confidently for what matters by giving your inner sage a powerful external voice. To help Emily find her true voice, I suggested that she use the imaginary soapbox technique (as in Exercise 17: Amplify Your True Voice, page 94), which provides a platform on which you can feel completely safe, confident and unjudged, and speak your true feelings without repercussion—no criticism or attacks.

When asked about her new assignment while on the imaginary soapbox, Emily replied, "My fiancé is more important. I do not want to take this assignment; I would rather keep my commitment to him." She also realized that she could manage without this client's assignments in general and would find other work to replace them.

Off of her soapbox, Emily remarked, "Wow, I felt so clear on there—no awkwardness, no fear, no need to explain myself or give in to their demands." The exercise made her feel powerful and allowed her inner sage an opportunity to speak clearly, without reservation.

Emily used the imaginary soapbox technique that day to call her agency and refuse the assignment. The call was not easy for her to make; it took great courage to face criticism, humiliation and fury, but she did it. By taking a stand for herself, Emily embraced her innate wisdom and protected her life happiness. She has been reaping the rewards ever since.

To give your inner sage center stage, complete Exercise 17: Amplify Your True Voice. Use this technique whenever you need help speaking your truth or bringing your inner sage's wisdom into the world. The more frequently you use it, the more quickly the truth will come to you when you need it. People who admire you will value your fortitude and clarity and may even follow your lead. Not everyone will be able to honor your truth, though; those people will not be your allies in building the life you love, and you will have to find a way to move forward without them.

EXERCISE 17:

Amplify Your True Voice

Without a doubt, your ability to honor yourself by speaking your truth will boost your long-term self-confidence. It will open doors for more honest conversations with people, potentially deepening and expanding those relationships.

→ To begin, find a private area where you will not be overheard or interrupted, like an office or bedroom with the door closed. Think of a situation in which you have been lying to someone or otherwise avoiding confrontation.

1. Stand comfortably. Relax and breathe deeply.
2. Look about 3 feet in front of you and imagine a 2-foot square outlined on the floor. (Or create a temporary square on the floor with chalk, masking tape, paper or whatever you have handy.) This square represents your soapbox. When you stand on it, you can speak freely without fear of judgment or reprisal.
3. Step onto your soapbox. Take a few quiet moments to consult your inner sage and get in touch with your deepest desires.
4. With confidence, state out loud how you honestly feel about the situation.

How does it feel to give your inner sage a voice? Write your thoughts in your YOLO journal.

After learning to speak with the voice of her inner sage, Emily began to refuse the unreasonable demands of her agency.

She later shared, "Because of finding my priorities and putting them first, those frustrating work requests became a good thing—stepping stones that helped me move out of the business altogether. I quit working with the agency. While I miss the extra cash, I certainly don't miss the heartaches and frustrations of missing family events."

Since then, Emily has married, started a new career, moved cross-country and had a beautiful baby boy.

No-Lie Policy

Don't you admire a person who can respond honestly to requests for their time? You can be that person who speaks gracefully and truthfully, with a bit of planning and practice!

To make it simpler to speak your truth, consider adopting a *no-lie policy,* which means always choosing not to fib, avoid or lie—to yourself or anyone else—no exceptions. The key guidelines to a no-lie policy are:

- Challenge yourself to stop before making a commitment, offer or agreement that you are not one hundred percent sure about.
- If necessary, ask for and take time to formulate your response.
- Consult your inner sage to identify your personal needs in the situation.
- Then, and only then, express your needs while respecting the situation and relationship by choosing your words deliberately.

You also must get comfortable with sometimes *asking for what you want* and *saying no* politely when needed. Most people are not as good at these two things as they would like to be. Remember that the truth rarely offends, particularly if phrased in first-person ("I") statements. For example, "No thank you, I deeply value making annual donations to three other charities that are important to me" could be a true and personal statement that is not as potentially inflammatory as "No, we don't want to donate to your cause."

Situations that involve the potential loss of an important relationship, money, status or security are especially difficult. To stick to your no-lie policy when you face these kinds of worries, you must:

- Identify your opportunity for happiness that is being threatened. *(In Emily's case, it was the chance to spend special time with her family.)*
- Understand the worries that might cause you to sacrifice your own happiness. *(Emily faced the threat of losing assignments and thus income from her agency.)*
- Compare these two options, and plan your response accordingly. *(Emily realized that her fiancé was more important and that she could find other work that was more in line with her priorities.)* Use the technique from Exercise 17: Amplify Your True Voice for help with this last step, if needed.

Complete Exercise 18: Practice a No-Lie Policy to start slowly; try speaking only your truth for a day, then a week, and finally an entire month. Living this way initially takes a little extra mental effort, but you will notice a big and immediate improvement in your quality of life.

EXERCISE 18:
Practice a No-Lie Policy

Start practicing a no-lie policy a little bit at a time!

→ For just one day this week, strive to speak your absolute truth. During (or at the end of) the day, list in your YOLO journal any difficult or surprising situations, along with your thoughts about how to handle similar situations in the future.

Then, schedule one full week during the next month to practice a no-lie policy. Mark these days as "NLP" on your calendar. Again, record your experiences and thoughts in your YOLO journal.

Finally, take out your calendar and choose one month from the next three when you will practice a no-lie policy for the entire month, still recording your experiences and thoughts. (**Note:** You may choose to build on the week you just completed.)

After one full month of enforcing your personal no-lie policy, you should have the skills to continue indefinitely.

If you're having trouble putting this policy into practice:

Start out more slowly, following the instructions in the exercise above but using a no-lie policy in certain situations only, like at home or among trusted friends. After you have practiced the no-lie policy in these situations for one month, review your experiences and thoughts, making note of your improvements and how your comfort level has changed over the month.

Repeat the exercise, using a no-lie policy in another situation. When you feel comfortable, repeat the exercise in all situations.

Helpful Hints

Your inner sage is always accessible and inexhaustible—you cannot tire it, wear it out or ask it too much. However, if you are eagerly or desperately trying to access it in a state of dismay or anxiety about a specific situation, the voice of your inner sage may be difficult to hear because your internal voices of worry and concern are louder and are drowning it out.

To quiet troubling voices or alleviate an anxiety, slow down, talk it out (with a friend or life coach) or engage in a rhythmic activity—walking, exercising or deep breathing. After your fears have quieted down, coast for a few minutes. Then sit alone and try tuning in to your inner sage again. You should have clearer access. **Note:** If you work with a friend or life coach, tell them to *ask you questions* (not give you advice!) so you can find your own answers.

When consulting your inner sage, do not, under any circumstances, derail yourself by saying, "I don't know." *You do know!* Rephrase the question until you reach your truth, which may be a specific answer or the realization that you need additional information before you can make a choice. Either option is valid.

Consult your inner sage for at least a few minutes each day. Remember, if you are not satisfied with your life, your inner sage is trying to tell you something—and it's time to start listening.

Now that you have learned to listen to your inner sage, you will begin making choices that are more in accord with what you deeply want and therefore are much more satisfying. In Step 3: Design Your Ideal Life, you'll translate what your inner sage tells you to a vision of your ideal life and goals for achieving it.

Design Your Ideal Life

FLAWED LOGIC ABOUT MONEY AND OTHER ISSUES CAN KEEP YOU FROM HAVING THE LIFE YOU WANT.
LEARN HOW TO BREAK FREE FROM FALSE ASSUMPTIONS, DISCOVER YOUR TRUE VALUES, CREATE A VISION OF YOUR IDEAL LIFE AND DEVELOP A PLAN FOR ACHIEVING IT.

When Harvard University sociologists asked people how much money they'd need to be "perfectly happy," rich and poor alike said twenty percent more than they currently have would do it.

-KAY MILLER[10]

Term Used in This Chapter

facets of life: the interconnected (and often interdependent) aspects of everyday human existence that affect life satisfaction; a useful framework to use for thoroughly designing an ideal life

10. Miller, Kay. 2003. America's Compulsive Consumption. *Minneapolis–St. Paul Star Tribune*, reprinted in *Portsmouth Herald*, Dec. 14, p. F1.

So far, you have built a foundation for dramatically changing your life. You know how to enjoy life by putting meaningful activities first, pause your mental agenda by coasting and consult your inner sage to find the answers to important life questions.

In Step 3: Design Your Ideal Life, you will learn how to uncover your true emotional desires even if they might be cloaked in false assumptions. Then, you will identify and describe the strongest, most consistent desires of your ideal life—the common threads that are woven through all of your favorite life moments. Next, you will refine the goals that will lead you there. Finally, you will create a game plan for achieving those goals and keep your most important desires at the top of your to-do list.

Step 3: Design Your Ideal Life is the central work of the You Only Live Once (YOLO) program. The more time and concentration you can give to these exercises, the more dramatic the change that you will create to improve your life. Even though this step appears to contain fewer exercises than the other chapters, these exercises are more involved and will take you longer to complete. For example, you will complete Exercise 21: Describe Your Ideal (for Each Facet), Exercise 22: Create Goals (for Each Facet) and Exercise 23: Develop Action Items (for Each Facet) separately for each of the Ten Facets of Your Ideal Life (page 111). Please plan to take your time and give adequate attention to each exercise to get the most benefit.

To dramatically change your life with the YOLO program, you must know all of the elements of the new life you want. Not sure what they are yet? Your inner sage knows—and so will you, after this step!

What You Really Want

The greatest revolution in our generation is the discovery that human beings, by changing the inner state of their minds, can change the outer aspects of their lives.

–William James

Many people can't create the life they love because their understanding of *what they really want* is buried beneath their assumptions about *what they think they want.* They may hold fast to seemingly logical conclusions that are based on false assumptions, be mired in other people's definitions of success or continue to pursue items that ultimately will not meet their emotional needs.

Your wishes are profound, and they are your only guide toward authentic happiness. As my coaching colleague Claudette Rowley has said to me many times when I've held back, "You are always allowed to want what you want!"

A Deeper Truth

A large part of my work involves helping people uncover what they really want. Over the years, many clients have told me that they wanted a boat, a trip around the world or a dream house. However, when asked what these items would bring them, their answers were usually something like, "connection with my kids," "downtime with my wife," "fun with my friends," "time to take care of myself" or "a chance to relax and unwind." They believed that the items (e.g., boat, trip or dream house)—and therefore the money required to obtain them—logically would lead to the desired emotional connections (e.g., with family, friends or self), when actually, the emotional connections were the deeper desires. For this reason, it is important to always ask yourself, "Is this item that I seek the only way to achieve the emotional outcome I desire, or am I limiting myself by believing that it is the only way to get what I want?"

My friend Noelle, a children's librarian, summed up this concept succinctly with a lesson she learned in library training: "People think they know what section of the library they need. They figure they have already done the logical thinking and just need to be pointed in the right direction. The reality is, when their assumptions are wrong, logic does not apply. For example, a patron asking for a book on the African lion could assume they need to look for a book in the section about Africa when what they really need is the section on animals." This statement is applicable to everything that you want in life, from finding the right library book to attaining your deepest happiness.

To understand just how common false assumptions are, consider what happened at a one-day time-management workshop that I once led for twenty-five male affiliates of an auto body repair association.

> *When asked what they would do if they had all the time in the world, the attendees' replies were consistent and comical: go fishing. When asked why they chose fishing, they volunteered more meaningful replies, like, "for quiet time alone" and "to spend more one-on-one time with my son."*
>
> *I asked the men, "When fishing is too difficult to arrange, what could you do to get some quiet time alone or spend some one-on-one time with your sons?" The room went silent as they wrote down their answers. Next, the men shared ideas with those sitting nearby. As their conversations gained momentum, their voices grew louder and more animated.*
>
> *Because the men were excited about their new ideas for getting what they wanted, I asked each one to make a commitment, in writing, to themselves, that they would try one of their new approaches* ***this week.*** *I instructed them to write and then fold up a helpful reminder about this commitment and place it in a shirt pocket or wallet—someplace where they were sure to stumble on it in the next twenty-four hours.*

The men left the workshop with a new tool for avoiding false assumptions (i.e., what they thought they wanted but couldn't have) and getting what they really wanted. Now it's your turn. Complete Exercise 19: Test Your Assumptions to learn how to avoid being pulled off track by false assumptions.

EXERCISE 19:

Test Your Assumptions

To make your best decisions, your thought process must be informed by facts and logic, not assumptions. Protect yourself against making leaps of judgment based on old patterns or habits by methodically examining and brainstorming each situation and option.

→ Think about a time when you noticed yourself saying, "I want..." or "If only I had..." Ask yourself the following questions, and write your answers in your YOLO journal.

1. **What I am trying to gain in this situation?**
2. **What will [the answer to question #1] give me or allow me to have?**
3. **What do I actually need to do to get [the answer to question #2]?**
4. **Am I exploring all the options for how I can have or do [the answer to question #3]?**
5. **Is there a way to accomplish [the answer to question #3] immediately, without waiting?**

Repeat this exercise anytime you think you may be taking the long road to your goals.

Being Successful

During each person's lifetime, parents, peers, society and especially advertising present expectations about how life should be. These expectations create a sort of yardstick with which to judge one's success and compare it with others'. The resulting illusion of "not measuring up" can lead to a problematic belief that more (of anything) is required to be happy. However, if you gauge your success by a measure that is based on someone else's idea of success, and your own idea of success is different, the conclusion will be a false assumption.

To distinguish what you truly desire from what others say you should have, you must develop your own definition of *success.* Clarifying what success means to you will help you make better decisions about how you spend your time and your resources. For instance, if you have young children, being a full-time stay-at-home parent might be of value to you. If you have a creative passion, working just enough to provide for your necessities may be ideal, so you have more time to develop your creativity. These choices are legitimate and only two of the myriad possible options.

If you feel that you are not succeeding in life, you have lost sight of what truly matters—not to others or to society, but to you—and no longer know what you need to be happy. The key to getting out of this trap and redesigning your life is to identify exactly what you want. You started this process in Step 2: Go Inward to Find Your Answers by getting to know your inner sage; now, clarify what you truly desire by completing Exercise 20: Define Success on Your Own Terms.

EXERCISE 20:
Define Success on Your Own Terms

You won't be able to get what you want from life if you never contemplate your own definition of success. It is time to give your inner sage center stage again!

⟶ Take a quiet moment to be alone with your inner sage. Ask yourself,

What makes me feel personally successful in life?

As you formulate your answer, some aspects to consider include:

- The state of your health
- The depth of your loving relationships
- Financial security
- Personal accomplishments
- How often you are kind
- The legacy you will leave behind

Also consider all of the roles you may play on any given day and how your ideas about success are reflected in those roles:

- Artist/creative person
- Employee/employer
- Friend
- Neighbor

- **Organization Member**
- **Parent**
- **Son/daughter**
- **Spouse/partner**
- **Student**
- **Volunteer**

In your YOLO journal, write as much about your feelings on success as you can.

After you have finished, go back and review what you have written. Highlight the key elements; they represent your personal definition of success. Rewrite them as numbered or bulleted points so they are easy to find and refer back to when you need to be reminded of what success means to you.

It's Not About the Money

Money is the answer to every problem and a sure route to happiness, right? Unfortunately, this is yet another false assumption. Even so, many of my clients over the years have blamed money for their problems: If only they had more of it, everything would be better and their lives would be happier.

Perhaps surprisingly, statistics tell another tale. According to a BBC News report, in the United Kingdom, "Despite large increases in national income (and expenditure) over the last thirty years, levels of life satisfaction have not increased commensurately."[11] Thus it appears that money *can't* buy happiness, even though many people spend their lives believing that it can.

11. Donovan and Halpern 2002.

The truth is that money is more likely to complicate problems than to solve them. Ironically, people strapped for time may buy items they hope will help them become more organized, accomplish more and feel less exhausted, but owning these items can make their lives more stressful because they have to manage and pay for them! How many times have you been thrilled to buy a new gadget, only to realize that it was going to take you hours to figure out how to use it or that it was not maintenance-free? Have you ever stretched your budget to buy something "helpful" only to cringe when you saw the charge on your credit card bill later?

The result of "money is the only way" thinking is that people end up spending extra hours working to earn money to buy things while sacrificing life's pleasures right now. Rather than waiting for a boat or a trip or a house that might be difficult to afford or you could be paying off for years, why not find a way to create more time with your children, feel closer to your partner or do something else that you love to do right now? You wouldn't be the only one choosing quality time over money.

According to a poll commissioned by the Center for a New American Dream in partnership with the organizers of Take Back Your Time Day (www.timeday.org), more than four out of five Americans surveyed (including adults with and without children) wished they had more time to spend with family. Furthermore, "More than half of Americans (52%) say they would be willing to trade a day off a week for a day's pay a week."[12] In other words, more than half of Americans surveyed would rather have *more time* than *more money.*

The following unattributed story about a Mexican fisherman came to me by email a long time ago, and I use it in many of my seminars. This parable perfectly illustrates the concepts of false assumptions, personal success and the value of money

12. Center for the New American Dream. 2004. *Take Back Your Time Poll: Americans Eager to Take Back Their Time.* Charlottesville, VA: Center for the New American Dream. www. Newdream.org/about/polls/timepoll.php

versus happiness, all of which are important to clarify when you're planning the route to the life you want.

An American investment banker was at the pier of a small coastal Mexican village when a fisherman docked his small boat which was loaded with several large yellow-fin tuna. The American complimented the fisherman on the quality of the fish and asked how long it took to catch them. The fisherman replied, "Only a little while."

When the American asked why he didn't stay out longer and catch more fish, the fisherman replied that he had enough to support his family's immediate needs. The American then asked, "But what do you do all day?" to which the fisherman replied, "I sleep late, fish a little, play with my children, take siestas with my wife and stroll into the village where I sip wine and play guitar with my amigos. I have a full and happy life."

The American scoffed, "I have a Masters in Business Administration and could help you. You should fish more and buy a bigger boat with the profits. With the profits from the bigger boat, you would buy several boats and eventually have a fleet. Instead of selling your catch to a middleman, you would sell directly to the processor and then open your own cannery. You would control the product, processing and distribution. You would leave this village and move to Mexico City, then Los Angeles and eventually New York, where you would run your expanding enterprise."

The fisherman asked, "How long will all this take?" to which the American replied, "Fifteen to twenty years."

The fisherman scratched his head and asked, "Then what?" The American laughed and replied, "When the time is right, you will announce an initial public offering (IPO) and sell your company stock to the public and become very rich; you will make millions!"

Still not convinced, the fisherman asked again, "Then what?"

Exasperated, the American explained: "You will retire—move to a small coastal fishing village where you will sleep late, fish a little, play with your kids, take siestas with your wife and stroll into the village where you will sip wine and play guitar with your friends."

This businessman displays the common belief that people must work hard, acquire lots of things and make a lot of money before they can have what they truly want. He does not recognize an ideal life when it's standing right in front of him! Why should the fisherman work hard for fifteen to twenty years before retiring to the lifestyle he already enjoys? All that extra work isn't necessary, and understanding that idea does not make him lazy or unsuccessful.

There are many ways to measure wealth and success, and like the fisherman already knows, you don't have to "make millions" to lead a full and happy life.

A young software programmer from Japan named Chou came to me for help with her career change. She wanted a fulfilling job that would give back to the world, so she had used logic to decide to become a nurse, but now felt unsure about her decision. (No doubt, her ambivalence was her inner sage nudging her to test her assumptions.)

On exploration, she realized that she indeed loved helping people navigate unfamiliar circumstances when they felt vulnerable; however, she really didn't have a strong passion for medicine itself. She did, however, have a talent for, and love of, languages. Working as a translator for an organization like the Red Cross was identified as a much more fulfilling career option for her that would meet her lifestyle choices, deeper objectives and her personal definition of success.

Ten Facets of Your Ideal Life

The future belongs to those who believe in the beauty of their dreams.

~Eleanor Roosevelt

Like a perfect crystal whose surfaces reflect a rainbow of color as you turn it in the light, a happy life presents many angles, or facets, from which to view it. This section will help you dramatically expand on your definition of success from Exercise 20: Define Success on Your Own Terms and identify all of the necessary elements to build the life you want. You will do this by systematically exploring ten aspects of human existence that affect life satisfaction. I call them the *facets of life* (pages 118-138):

1. Family
2. Friends
3. Home
4. Work
5. Finances
6. Health
7. Talent
8. Personal Growth
9. Spirituality
10. Community

Home

Work

HEALTH

FINANCES

Friends

The 10 Facets

Family

Personal Growth

Spirituality

Talent

COMMUNITY

These ten categories may look deceivingly simple and familiar, but don't be fooled. As you work your way through each one in depth, you will build the thorough framework needed to identify what you really want in every area of your life. This system ensures you do not miss any particular component and also makes certain that you consider your life as a whole.

These facets are ultimately interconnected and often interdependent, so it is important to consider each and every one. At the end of this step, you will be able to clearly evaluate the sum of the parts: a complete plan for a new and dramatically improved life.

How to Proceed

This section contains three exercises that will guide you through:

- Describing the ten facets as they relate to your vision of an ideal life
- Creating goals that will help you achieve your ideal future
- Developing action items for making your vision a reality

The Ten Facets of Your Ideal Life are described in detail (pages 118-138) and presented with prompts and questions to guide your introspection in general and help you complete Exercise 21: Describe Your Ideal (for Each Facet) in particular. Some facet descriptions also include ideas for addressing special cases in which you desire change.

Work on one facet at a time, completing Exercises 21–23 for that facet before moving on to the next facet. Plan to work on each facet in at least one-hour increments (longer if you can), because you will need this much time to slow down and process your thoughts. This methodical approach will keep your inner sage focused and provide the clearest, most thorough answers for each category.

You do not have to approach the facets in the sequence I present them. Feel free to address the facets in the order they speak to you. However, **complete all the facets—especially the ones you would prefer to avoid.** All ten facets have important information to reveal to you about the quality of the life you wish to create, even if you don't think so. And because the facets are interconnected, you will need to work through all of them to create a *complete* design for your future.

Before you begin these exercises, I suggest that you review your answers from Exercise 14: Flash Forward to Discover What Really Matters (page 81) and Exercise 15: Consult Your Inner Sage (page 84) from Step 2: Go Inward to Find Your Answers. It will be helpful to have this information fresh in your mind as you create a new plan for your life.

After you finish all of the exercises for a facet, share your findings with a loved one, friend or coach. Revisit a completed facet at any time to update or add to it as life events occur or your circumstances change. You may also add facets to the list that are specific to your life and then use Exercise 21: Describe Your Ideal (for Each Facet), Exercise 22: Create Goals (for Each Facet) and Exercise 23: Develop Action Items (for Each Facet) to probe for additional essential information.

Note: Do not proceed to Step 4 until you have completed Exercises 21–23 for all ten facets.

EXERCISE 21:
Describe Your Ideal (for Each Facet)

To begin, slow down—sit in the sun, tuck into a corner of a coffee shop or relax in your favorite armchair—and be alone and undisturbed with this book, your YOLO journal and your thoughts.

Select the facet you wish to work on, and write it at the top of a blank page in your YOLO journal. **Note:** As you work through the rest of the exercises for Step 3: Design Your Ideal Life, organize entries in your YOLO journal by facet, then by exercise number and question number (if appropriate), because you will return to some of your answers in subsequent exercises.

→ Read the description of the facet you chose and its relevant questions in the sections that follow Exercise 23, then reflect on what it means to you personally. Take your time; sit quietly and engage in a powerful conversation with your inner sage to find your wisest answers. When your feelings about this facet are clear, honestly answer the questions included in the facet description in your YOLO journal and add any additional thoughts or realizations.

After you complete this exercise for your chosen facet, proceed to Exercise 22: Create Goals (for Each Facet), continuing to work with this same facet.

EXERCISE 22:

Create Goals (for Each Facet)

Now that you have described your ideals for this facet of life, refine the goals that you would like to achieve in this area. These goals will help you create opportunities for bringing these ideals to life.

→ Ask yourself the following questions, and write your answers for this facet in your YOLO journal:

1. How do I want my description of this facet to be different one year from today?
2. What do I need more of right now to achieve [the answer to question #1] during the next year?
3. How will having [the answer to question #2] bring me happiness?
4. What do I need less of right now to have more of [the answer to question #2]?
5. How will not having [the answer to question #4] make me happier?
6. At this point in my life, what three accomplishments related to this facet am I most proud of?
7. What do [the answer to question #6] tell me about who I am and what I believe I can achieve?
8. Which people do I value most in my life related to this facet?

9. What is something related to this facet that I have always wanted to do but haven't yet?

10. How do I want my description of this facet to be different five years from today?

After you complete this exercise for your chosen facet, proceed to Exercise 23: Develop Action Items (for Each Facet), continuing to work with this same facet.

EXERCISE 23:

Develop Action Items (for Each Facet)

Your answers to the following questions will transform your goals from Exercise 22: Create Goals (for Each Facet) into action items with specific due dates. The idea is to create dramatic change by planning for consistent progress; each small step forward will bring you closer to the life you want!

→ Refer back to your answers to Exercise 22: Create Goals (for Each Facet), questions #2, #4 and #9, for the facet you are working on. Ask yourself the following questions and write your answers in your YOLO journal in the same section allocated for that facet.

1. Is this goal realistic and achievable? *(Brainstorm all the variables that might get in the way of reaching your goal (e.g., distance, technology concerns, work schedules, home duties and other demands on your time) and determine whether each variable is realistic in the context of your life and, if not, how you can make it so. If any goal is not realistic, it is also not achievable; revise it until it is.)*

2. What must I do to achieve this goal completely? *(List specific action items for achieving this goal with due dates within the next twelve months.)*

After you have completed this exercise for one facet, return to Exercise 21: Describe Your Ideal (for Each Facet) and start working on another facet.

Repeat this process until you have worked through Exercises 21–23 for all ten facets.

Facet 1. Family

Put simply, any given person's family includes all manner of loved ones. They are not necessarily your blood relatives, rather they are the nearest and dearest people in your life.

Your family, however defined, is your most immediate source of support. Clarify who you wish to call "family" and what they mean to you. Consider what you expect from your family in terms of emotional, practical or financial support and what you believe your contribution to your family should be.

After you take some time to consult your inner sage, ask yourself the following questions and write your answers in your YOLO journal for Exercise 21: Describe Your Ideal (for Each Facet).

- How do I define *family*? Immediate or extended family? Biological, adopted or chosen family?
- Who is part of my family?
- Who in my family is difficult to get along with or be around?
- Within my family, which relationships would I like to be different, and in what ways? Do I want some to be deeper? Do I need clearer boundaries to distance and protect myself?
- How do I want to contribute to my family—for instance, do I need to be in touch more? Is it time to arrange a long-distance visit or schedule a regular time to make phone calls?
- When was the last time I hosted or attended a family gathering? Does this idea appeal to me?

To Find a Special Someone

Identify the top five characteristics you would like in your ideal partner. Also reflect on past relationships. What did they lack that you desire in a future relationship? Do you need to resolve any unanswered issues before you can begin with someone new?

To Evaluate a Loving Relationship

Step back and evaluate the success of your union. Are you satisfied emotionally, intellectually and physically? If so, does your relationship need more priority in your life? If not, how could you improve and honor the importance of this relationship? If you are dissatisfied with your partnership, consider seeking couples counseling or moving on, because you both deserve to be in a fully satisfying relationship with someone who meets your needs.

To Set Boundaries with a Family Member

Spending time with someone who makes you feel uncomfortable, annoyed, defensive or angry will slow your progress toward your ideal life. The negativity generated by this relationship will detract from your overall happiness. Addressing such problems with family members can be especially difficult, because other people who are important to you will be affected by your words, actions and decisions. However difficult the situation appears, remember why you're trying to change the situation: to improve your life. And who knows, maybe your experience will inspire a relative to change their tune, if not their life, too!

First, identify exactly how the relationship drains you. (Does this person demand your presence at holiday gatherings? Belittle you? Tell you how to raise your child? Act in a way that you consider inappropriate? Make unreasonable demands on your time?) Next, brainstorm some ways to potentially alleviate or eliminate the effects of this behavior on your well-being. (**Note:** Include actions you can take as well as actions to suggest to your relative.) When you feel confident that you can explain your problem and suggested solution(s) calmly and clearly, approach the family member. Begin by emphasizing their importance to your family, and if you honestly care for them, remind them that you do. Explain your problem, using objective terms and "I" statements and potential solution(s). (**Note:** The emphasis must be on *how you feel*—not only *how they act*—to avoid an accusatory tone that provokes a defensive reaction.) For example, if a particular relative always hosts holiday gatherings but you would like to try something different, explain that you understand that they like to have the family together but would like to take a turn hosting (or travel, or spend time with someone else who has been inviting you for years). If you find a relative's behavior or comments inappropriate, explain exactly what you take issue with and how it affects you, then suggest how they might act differently (e.g., "When you criticize my political choices, it makes me feel unwelcome; I would prefer that we no longer discuss politics at family gatherings.").

Depending on the situation, you may announce what you intend to do or suggest coming up with a compromise together. If your relative is unwilling to accept or comply with your request(s), reexamine your issues and brainstorm another boundary. If all else fails, avoid situations in which the person who bothers you will be present so you can cultivate, not sabotage, your happiness.

Facet 2. Friends

Friendships are one of life's greatest gifts. Close friends are supportive in good times and bad, help celebrate big and small accomplishments, and share joy as well as pain. Even casual acquaintances add connection and camaraderie to life.

You must clarify how many and what kinds of friendships fit into your vision of an ideal life. (You may wish to break this facet into several smaller categories, for example, inner circle [five or six closest buddies], work colleagues, acquaintances [this group may be quite large] and new friends you wish to make.) Think carefully about how your friendships enhance or detract from your life, and use this information to build a positive, supportive network while eliminating negative relationships.

After you take some time to consult your inner sage, ask yourself the following questions and write your answers in your YOLO journal for Exercise 21: Describe Your Ideal (for Each Facet).

- Am I satisfied with my current friendships? Why or why not?
- What would make me feel satisfied? More friends? Deeper connections with the friends I already have? What can I do to create this change?
- Who are my closest friends?
- Do I receive enough of the joy that deep friendship brings?
- Describe an ideal friend. What characteristics do they possess that enhance my life? What personality traits are appealing?
- Are any friendships draining me? If so, how?

To Deepen a Friendship

Arrange to spend more time with this person. When you feel a connection, share something important to you with them—perhaps one of your new goals or a situation you are trying to change—and ask for their ideas. By collaborating, even just in conversation, your bond will grow closer.

To Expand Your Circle of Friends

Join a club, volunteer or take a class doing something you love; you will meet like-minded folks and enjoy a favorite activity at the same time.

To Set Boundaries with a Friend

Friendships naturally change over time as interests, situations and life goals change; they may even quietly fade away as the parties grow in different directions. If at any point a friend saps your energy or makes you feel uncomfortable, annoyed or angry, you should take action to improve the situation. The negativity generated by such a relationship will detract from your overall happiness and slow your progress toward your ideal life.

First identify exactly how the friendship drains you. Next, brainstorm some ways to potentially alleviate or eliminate the negative effects on your well-being. (**Note:** Include actions you can take as well as actions to suggest to your friend.) When you feel confident that you can explain your problem and suggested solution(s) calmly and clearly, approach your friend. Begin by emphasizing their importance in your life, and if you honestly care for them, remind them that you do. Explain your problem, using objective terms and "I" statements and potential solution(s). (**Note:** The emphasis must be on *how you feel*—not only *how they act*—to avoid an accusatory tone that provokes a defensive reaction.) For example, if a friend typically calls when you're busy or tired, tell them what times you tend to be most available to talk or that you prefer not to receive phone calls after a certain time. If a friend tends to go on and on about their troubles, explain that you would like to strive for more balance in your sharing or put a time limit on your visits.

When you enforce your new boundary (perhaps with a couple of reminders), you can expect this person to either change their behavior because they see the value in keeping your friendship, or look elsewhere because they no longer get what they need from you. Either way, problem solved.

Facet 3. Home

Home can be an oasis from the outside world, a haven for recharging from over-exertion or recovering from illness, a launching pad for outside adventures, a stage for entertaining or a protected space for belongings. In a larger context, it should also take into account desires about type of neighborhood, transportation options, and proximity to people, places and things that are important.

Think about what makes your space feel like home for you. Plants? A cozy nook for reading? Easy access to cultural events? Creating an ideal home does not necessarily require relocation or expense. Sometimes rearranging furniture, decorating with meaningful objects and photographs, or removing clutter can make a striking difference.

After you take some time to consult your inner sage, ask yourself the following questions and write your answers in your YOLO journal for Exercise 21: Describe Your Ideal (for Each Facet).

- What would my ideal home feel like? How does this ideal differ from where I currently reside?
- Am I a city dweller, a suburbanite or a country person?
- What do I like to do at home? Does my current living situation support those activities?
- How do I describe my home space? Clean or dirty? Tidy or messy? Minimalist or cluttered? Or some combination of these descriptions, depending on the room?
- How does my current home space make me feel? Calm and centered? Scattered and unfocused? Somewhere in between, depending on the room?

- Do I wish I lived closer to family? Friends? Work? The mountains? Somewhere else?
- Do I have easy access to activities I enjoy?

To Clear Your Space

When you declutter and organize, you open up space—literally and figuratively—for new opportunities to come into your life. Your actions give the universe the signal that you can manage what you have and are ready for more. If your space—home, office or room—could be described as anything from untidy to chaotic, reclaim your power over that space to find the inner calm that will support your progress in the YOLO program.

Do an Internet search on "clutter" or "declutter" and find blogs and articles that list the basics of this task. (A good rule of thumb is, if something hasn't been used in the past six months and doesn't contribute to your happiness, you probably don't need it!) FlyLady (www.flylady.net) is one popular site that offers common-sense advice to help you learn to organize and declutter your life. One book I have found helpful is *Organizing from the Inside Out,* a practical step-by-step guide to imposing order on your surroundings.[13] If you need additional help cleaning up and clearing out, hire a professional organizer who will guide you through this process.

> *Gary was a client of mine who left a corporate accounting job to pursue his dreams of being his own boss and playing French horn.*
>
> *At one point, Gary lived in a Philadelphia townhouse where it was difficult to practice music due to the proximity of his neighbors. When we discussed this problem in the context of his larger life vision, Gary revealed that he had*

13. Morgenstern, Julie. 2004. *Organizing from the Inside Out: The Foolproof System for Organizing Your Home, Your Office, and Your Life* (2nd ed.). New York: Henry Holt.

always wanted to live near the sea. We explored many solutions, from working out a schedule with neighbors to moving to a new area.

Ultimately, Gary met both ideals, along with other long-held life goals, by making a dramatic relocation. He moved to a bungalow in San Francisco where he could practice his French horn without concern and be at the seashore in minutes.

Facet 4. Work

Work is any regular (daily or not) vocation, whether that vocation is a stay-at-home parent, a cattle rancher, a salesperson, an accountant in a two-person office, a factory worker or an astronaut in a national space program. Enjoyable work is an essential element of an ideal life because most people spend most of their awake time working.

Think about your work and why you do what you do. Are your reasons still as valid as when you began? What interested you years ago may no longer interest you. It's okay to explore options, within your career field and elsewhere. Be sure to consider all aspects of your working life, from the mundane (e.g., wardrobe and commute) to the fantasy (e.g., the dream job or promotion). Your work may provide financial security but also represents part of your personal contribution to the world. Make it worth your effort!

After you take some time to consult your inner sage, ask yourself the following questions and write your answers in your YOLO journal for Exercise 21: Describe Your Ideal (for Each Facet).

- What about my work makes me happy? Feeling a sense of pride or accomplishment? Receiving accolades or awards from my peers? Bringing home a paycheck? Feeling valued or appreciated by my family, colleagues, employer or customers? A sense of group camaraderie? Working as part of a team?

- How do I want to be compensated for my skills?
- Am I satisfied with my current financial compensation, if any (e.g., pay level, vacation time, bonus plan and other incentives)?
- What are my personal goals in my current position? What would I like to achieve?
- What is the next level I wish to attain in my work or career? Do I need additional training or qualifications to reach that goal?
- What would I change about my work if I could? Different hours? A shorter commute? Work from home a couple of days a week?
- Do I enjoy my work environment? Co-workers? Superiors?

To Change Careers

If your soul-searching leads you to change careers, know that the process requires serious introspection and effort, but it's certainly doable. First, become familiar with your innate talents and occupational temperament by taking a comprehensive, objective test of natural abilities (e.g., Highland's Natural Ability Battery, available via my website at www.vip-coaching.com). Next, examine your life thoroughly to trace your core values, passions and desires from childhood through today. With my clients, I use an assessment tool that I developed called the Life Experience Inventory. (**Note:** All of these resources are also listed in Online Resources at the end of this book.) Finally, use the results of these efforts to distill a short list of ideal careers that use your unique talents and fulfill your sense of purpose. After this profile is complete, you can address the practical aspects of a career search (e.g., salary, job security, retraining, position availability, and application and interview procedures).

One book that might help you through this process is the classic *What Color Is Your Parachute,* which has been revised annually for 35 years.[14] Another is *Don't Waste Your Talent* (written by the people who developed the Highland's Natural Ability Battery), which teaches you to harness your natural gifts.[15] If you desire one-on-one guidance, a trained life coach or career counselor can assist you with this process.

Facet 5. Finances

Money plays an important role in life. It allows people to procure the necessities for survival (food, shelter and clothing). It also provides a sense of security in regard to anticipated and unanticipated needs and taking care of loved ones. Each person chooses how to use this tool in their life.

Your ideas about finances may be shaped by your upbringing or a significant personal experience. Did you grow up always needing more money? Usually having enough to get by? Never having to worry about money? Did you lose a job once and struggle to make ends meet until you found a new one? Do you still embrace that perspective today even though your situation may be different?

Results of the World Giving Index 2010 (a 153-country Gallup poll about how much time and money people donate around the world) indicate "more correlation between happiness and giving than between wealth and giving."[16] In other words, happier people donate more of their resources, in both time and money. I think that logic works in the other direction, as well—people who share their resources tend to feel happier. Regardless of your current financial situation, do-

14. Bolles, Richard Nelson. 2009. *What Color Is Your Parachute? A Practical Manual for Job-Hunters and Career-Changers.* Berkeley, CA: Ten Speed Press.
15. Hutcheson, Don, and Bob McDonald. 2000. *Don't Waste Your Talent: The 8 Critical Steps to Discovering What You Do Best.* Atlanta, GA: Longstreet Press.
16. Jones, Clayton. 2010. Gallup Poll: Degree of One's Charity Depends on Happiness More Than Wealth. *Christian Science Monitor's* Editorial Board blog, Sept. 10. www.csmonitor.com/Commentary/Editorial-Board-Blog/2010/0910/Gallup-poll-Degree-of-one-s-charity-depends-on-happiness-more-than-wealth

nating even a few dollars to a cause that is important to you can be extremely rewarding and reinforce your feelings of abundance, knowing that you have enough to share.

Money can be a source of comfort or never-ending worry. Get your financial house in order if you need to. Make the necessary changes so you can focus your energies on achieving your goals, not worrying about finances.

After you take some time to consult your inner sage, ask yourself the following questions and write your answers in your YOLO journal for Exercise 21: Describe Your Ideal (for Each Facet).

- What does a satisfying life look like to me from a financial perspective?
- Do I feel comfortable with my current money situation? If not, what do I need to have in place to feel secure? An aggressive savings plan? Control on spending? A strategy to get out of debt?
- Would it be wise to consult a financial advisor who can guide me in retirement or estate planning?
- Would charitable giving make me feel happy? If so, what kind of giving will reflect my personal values?
- Do I need a simplified or automated system to manage my bills and plan for taxes?

If you spend more than you earn, you must determine the real issue. Do you need to spend less or earn more? Lack of money should not be a roadblock keeping you from what your inner sage truly desires. To find the root cause, go back to your answers to Exercise 19: Test Your Assumptions to be absolutely certain about what you really want—and whether money can buy it.

To Reduce Your Expenses or Debt

If you decide to reduce expenses so that you can live without the pressure of needing more money, I highly recommend *Your Money or Your Life,* which will teach you a new way of looking at money based on your true values.[17] If you need to reduce debt so you can have more options, I suggest *How to Get Out of Debt, Stay Out of Debt and Live Prosperously,* a step-by-step guide to help you change your relationship with credit.[18] I also recommend Suzy Orman's exercise (in *The 9 Steps to Financial Freedom*) of tracking your income and expenses for a month (or more) to see how accurate your assumptions are.[19]

To Increase Your Income

If you decide that you need to increase your income, you have options! Ask your employer for a salary increase or merit bonus for work well done, charge more for your services, take in a boarder or roommate, start a hobby business or broaden the market for your existing business, advance your qualifications or make a job change. See *Making a Living Without a Job*[20] for more ideas and *The One Minute Millionaire*[21] for inspiration.

17. Dominguez, Joe, and Vicki Robin. 1992. *Your Money or Your Life: Transforming Your Relationship with Money and Achieving Financial Independence.* New York: Viking.
18. Mundis, Jerrold. 2003. *How to Get Out of Debt, Stay Out of Debt and Live Prosperously.* New York: Bantam Books.
19. Orman, Suzy. 2006. *The 9 Steps to Financial Freedom: Practical and Spiritual Steps So You Can Stop Worrying* (updated and revised 3rd edition). New York: Three Rivers Press.
20. Winter, Barbara J. 2009. *Making a Living Without a Job: Winning Ways for Creating Work That You Love* (revised edition). New York: Bantam Books.
21. Hansen, Mark Victor, and Robert G. Allen. 2002. *The One Minute Millionaire: The Enlightened Way to Wealth* (1st edition). New York: Harmony Books.

Facet 6. Health

Many people do not take responsibility for their own health. They procrastinate about annual check-ups and avoid preventive procedures and care. They eat junk food and don't exercise consistently or get enough rest. They claim, "I don't have time to work out or cook!" Interestingly, the people who exercise and eat well are just as busy as everyone else. The difference is that they prioritize their health; they simply make different decisions.

Health ought to be your top-priority facet. Health is intimately interconnected with the other nine facets, and without it, your ideals for the other facets will be unattainable. So if your health needs improvement, be sure to put it at the top of your to-do list.

After you take some time to consult your inner sage, ask yourself the following questions and write your answers in your YOLO journal for Exercise 21: Describe Your Ideal (for Each Facet).

- What does "healthy" mean to me?
- Do I exercise regularly? Am I pleased with my fitness level?
- How many hours do I sleep each night? Is it enough? Do I regularly have trouble falling asleep?
- Are the foods I eat most often healthy? Is mealtime an opportunity to nourish my body or a quick stop at a drive-through window?
- Do I have any existing conditions that require periodic medical checkups? If so, am I vigilant about taking care of this aspect of my health?

- Do I know my important health statistics (e.g., weight, blood pressure, pulse, cholesterol and glucose levels)?
- Do I feel overly anxious? Lethargic? Disconnected? Depressed? Would it be useful to consult with a therapist about any of these issues?
- Am I pleased with my overall health? If not, how can I achieve my own definition of healthy, and what changes can I make so I can get the rest, exercise, care and nourishing food I need—so that health will no longer be a worry on my mental agenda?

To Make Healthier Food Choices

Two books that I found helpful for learning about and developing an appreciation for nutrition and how the human body works are *YOU: On a Diet*[22] and *Nutrition for Dummies.*[23] Both contain fascinating nuts-and-bolts details presented in a language that's easy for non-experts to understand. A free online resource to help count calories is The Daily Plate (www.TheDailyPlate.com). If you tend to use food as a coping mechanism, *Women Food and God* may help you overcome emotional eating habits.[24]

Facet 7. Talent

The need to use one's natural talent is an often-overlooked but essential component of happiness. When successfully absorbed in an activity that feels like an extension of yourself, you experience true bliss. Expressing innate talent is intimately connected to personal happiness and relaxation, and can also encourage coasting moments.

22. Roizen, Michael F., and Mehmet C. Oz, with Ted Spiker, Lisa Oz, and Craig Wynett. 2009. *YOU: On a Diet—The Owner's Manual for Waist Management* (revised, updated ed.). New York: Free Press.

23. Rinzler, Carol Ann. 2006. *Nutrition for Dummies* (4th ed.). Indianapolis, IN: Wiley.

24. Roth, Geneen. 2010. *Women Food and God: An Unexpected Path to Almost Everything.* New York: Simon & Schuster.

What is your natural talent? It's an activity that you are passionate about, enjoy and do well. If you think you don't have a talent, ask your mother, best friend or partner—they can tell you what it is! Then, if your talent is singing, join a chorus; if it's cooking, plan a dinner party; if it's karate, work toward the next belt. Do whatever makes you feel gifted; the pleasure you feel while doing it is what matters.

My most satisfied clients find that a key element in living a life they love is learning to make time for their talent—amateur photography, writing, sports, quilting, soap making, golfing, caring for others or operating a ham radio. Give your talent priority, and you will be rewarded with a deep sense of life satisfaction hard to find anywhere else. Not to mention, the world needs your talent. Imagine a world in which Picasso had never painted and Julia Child had never learned to cook—think of what humanity would have lost! Even if you do not compare yourself to such masters, your talent is a worthy contribution to those who can appreciate it.

After you take some time to consult your inner sage, ask yourself the following questions and write your answers in your YOLO journal for Exercise 21: Describe Your Ideal (for Each Facet).

- What do I love to do?
- What awards have I won? What accomplishments make me the most proud?
- What am I naturally good at? What comes as innately to me as breathing?
- When and how could I use my talents more?

To Unblock Your Talent

If you would like to encourage your creativity and develop your talent(s), I recommend *The Artist's Way.*[25] This classic book (originally published in 1992) is "a

25. Cameron, Julia. 2002. *The Artist's Way: A Spiritual Path to Higher Creativity* (10th anniversary ed.). New York: J. P. Tarcher/Putnam.

course in discovering and recovering your creative self," providing tools that will enhance any endeavor in which you're trying to tap into your creativity. (It's not only for visual artists!) Visit The Artist's Way Online (www.theartistsway.com) for additional information and resources related to the course, including a free online discussion forum.

Facet 8. Personal Growth

Most people already have a mental list of disciplines or activities they would love to pursue when they find the time—say, studying a foreign language, learning a new craft or working toward a professional certification. Planning a path (or several) of personal development is important, because improving one's mind or body allows for the investigation—and experience—of new possibilities for joy, pride and passion.

First, identify an area for personal growth (or two). If you are at a loss for ideas, gather magazines or catalogs around the house and clip images that inspire you. When you are finished, create a collage by taping the pictures to a wall, the front of your refrigerator or a large sheet of paper. What themes do you see? What excites you?

Next, scan your local adult education catalogs for classes and consult neighborhood bulletin boards for activities that stir your imagination. Magazine racks at bookstores and libraries are great for providing ideas and inspiration, too. Invite a friend to join you, if you wish.

After you take some time to consult your inner sage, ask yourself the following questions and write your answers in your YOLO journal for Exercise 21: Describe Your Ideal (for Each Facet).

- What topics have I been longing to explore?
- What new skill have I been itching to learn? How to knit? Scuba dive? Sell real estate?
- Would I like to broaden any existing talents (identified in the Talent facet)? If so, what would be the next step, and how can I get there?

Facet 9. Spirituality

Some level of spirituality is a key component of happiness for everyone, and it doesn't equate with membership in a religious organization. Spirituality is any practice that temporarily connects a person to something bigger than themselves—God, fate, a divine order, natural evolution or whatever it may be. It may mean appreciating the beauty of icicles melting in the winter sun or sitting in deep meditation searching for a direct experience of God. Any which way, personally inspiring experiences bring peace, hope and joy.

How do you experience spirituality? By attending weekly prayer services? Using your time and talents to help others? Taking a walk in nature? Meditating? Quietly contemplating life? Focusing on gratitude? Whatever it is for you, spirituality deserves as much attention, if not more, than other facets. Understanding and finding ways to connect with your deepest beliefs will give you a feeling of being in sync with the world as you see it. This sense of harmony offers opportunities to experience profound serenity.

After you take some time to consult your inner sage, answer the relevant lists of questions below in your YOLO journal for Exercise 21: Describe Your Ideal (for Each Facet) according to your beliefs.

For everyone:

- Where did humankind come from?
- Where do humans go after they die?
- Why do humans exist on earth; for what purpose?

For those who belong to an organized religious or spiritual group:

- Do I participate? Do I wish I participated more or less often? Do I want to be more involved as a volunteer or worker?
- What do I seek as a member of my spiritual community? What would I like to give back to this community?

For those who do not belong to an organized religious or spiritual group:

- How do I describe my own spiritual belief system? Does it have a name?
- What are the spiritual beliefs of my closest friends, family members or other people I admire? Do I share their beliefs?
- Do I believe in the existence (theist) or absence (atheist) of a god or gods, or am I unsure about the existence of a deity (agnostic)? Do I believe in the intangible or supernatural (metaphysics)? Do I believe that all people are inherently good or that the divine exists in all humans (humanist)? Do I believe in the divinity of nature?

To Find a Spiritual Community

One way to find a spiritual community is to shop around, attending different spiritual services or meetings in your area. Most churches and spiritual groups welcome visitors. Another option is to take a class in world religions to give you a high-level overview, then make a more targeted search in the areas that interest you.

To Create an Untraditional Spiritual Practice

Identify the activities that feel spiritual to you (e.g., walking in nature, writing, meditating or playing music) and schedule a weekly time with yourself to do these things in a tranquil, reflective manner. This practice offers a wonderful opportunity to coast, consider the world in a larger context, or touch base with your inner sage.

If you'd like to learn to meditate, *Lunchtime Enlightenment* provides instructions for incorporating this practice into daily life, whether you have five minutes or an hour.[26] The author, Pragito Dove, also offers free weekly meditations by email; sign up at her website (www.discovermeditation.com). If you would like to read about other people's personal experiences of the divine, I recommend *A Return to Love,*[27] which explores the relationship between God and love—of self and of others—and suggests how to view various aspects of life through the lens of spirituality; *Conversations with God,*[28] which explores the concept that there is no separation between humans and the divine; and *Here If You Need Me,*[29] a beautifully written, moving memoir that offers insightful explorations about life, death, God and love.

---

26. Dove, Pragito. 2001. *Lunchtime Enlightenment: Modern Meditations to Free the Mind and Unleash the Spirit—at Work, at Home, at Play.* New York: Viking Compass.
27. Williamson, Marianne. 1996. *A Return to Love: Reflections on the Principles of "A Course in Miracles."* New York: HarperCollins.
28. Walsch, Neale Donald. 1996. *Conversations with God: An Uncommon Dialogue.* (Book 1). Charlottesville, VA: Hampton Roads.
29. Braestrup, Kate. *Here If You Need Me: A True Story* (1st ed.). New York: Little, Brown and Co., 2007.

Facet 10. Community

To extend one's talents beyond oneself is important. It creates a sense of shared achievement and personal connection, and fulfills a basic human need to be a member of a social group. As an added bonus, this affiliation creates a supportive network of people one can call upon in times of need; it is called *community*.

To create your personal definition of *community*, recall experiences that have given you that good feeling of joining with others in pursuit of a common cause. Have you ever contributed to a large project as part of a group (perhaps a nonprofit event, car wash or theatrical production)? Volunteered at a local soup kitchen or festival? Canvassed for a political campaign? These experiences that made you feel proud to be connected to something bigger than yourself define your idea of community and represent good ways to become more involved in the future.

As you reflect on these experiences, be sure to also include one-to-one contributions that benefit individuals in your community:

- Assisting or visiting an elderly neighbor from time to time
- Delivering a home-cooked meal to a sick neighbor or a family with a new baby
- Picking up trash in a neighborhood park
- Contributing talent, time or money to a cause you support

Being part of a community should fill your spirit, not exhaust you. Approach these endeavors with the intention of achieving a healthy balance so you don't commit too much of your time or end up waiting on the sidelines. Believe it or not, both overcommitting and nonparticipation can lead to feelings of mental exhaustion. Whereas overcommitting can make you feel stretched to or beyond your limits, nonparticipation may lead to feelings of guilt. However you decide to participate, keep your level of involvement in line with the core values that you will identify below. If your participation starts to become an unwanted obligation, change it!

After you take some time to consult your inner sage, ask yourself the following questions and write your answers in your YOLO journal for Exercise 21: Describe Your Ideal (for Each Facet).

- Who do I consider part of my community? Friends? Neighbors? Teammates? Those connected with a social activity? Those connected with my children's school? Members of a club or community organization? My church?
- What level of interaction do I wish to have with these or other people in my community?
- Do I enjoy being part of an organization? If so, which types of organizations appeal to me? Social clubs? Athletic teams? Spiritual groups? Civic committees? Community theatre? If not, what kinds of personal connections interest me?
- How can my talents best be used in my community?

Getting There, One Step at a Time

Let me tell you the secret that has led to my goal: My strength lies solely in my tenacity.

-Louis Pasteur

Now that you have completed the three comprehensive exercises for all Ten Facets of Your Ideal Life, your YOLO journal includes many pages of descriptions, goals and action items for achieving those goals. Whether you feel overwhelmed (unsure what to do next) or excited (inspired to move full speed ahead) by all this information, **you must be absolutely sure about what you're working toward so you can plot your path.**

Your Vision

Whether planning a vacation or a dramatic life change, you must know where you're going before you can begin moving in the right direction! Because you have generated such a large quantity of powerful information about your beliefs and desires, I'll guide you through creating a short version that you can internalize and return to periodically to remind yourself what you're working toward. This summary—that is, your vision of your ideal life—does not need to be extremely detailed, because general statements will remind you of specific details that you consider important. However, each of the Ten Facets of Your Ideal Life must be represented.

Complete Exercise 24: Clarify Your Vision to distill all of the important information generated from the exercises in this chapter into a clear, concise, easily understood (and communicated) vision of your ideal life.

EXERCISE 24:
Clarify Your Vision

To clarify and clearly state your vision of the life you want to live, summarize your goals for each of the Ten Facets of Your Ideal Life.

→ To begin, turn to a blank page in your YOLO journal. Write numbers 1 to 10 along the left margin, leaving a couple of blank lines between each entry.

1. Keeping track of your current page, turn back to your notes for the first facet you worked on in Step 3: Design Your Ideal Life, and reread your answers to questions #1, #9 and #10 from Exercise 22: Create Goals (for Each Facet). Next to the first number, write the facet name, then write a one-sentence summary of your short-term goals for this facet (from the answer to question #1), what you want to do (from the answer to question #9) and your long-term goals (from the answer to question #10) that conveys the essence of your desires for this facet.

2. Continue to the next number in your list and repeat this exercise for the next facet until you have created ten summary statements.

3. Review all ten statements (for the ten facets), then revise any that are too wordy or don't truly reflect your desires. Copy the entire list to a new page if they aren't easy to read.

Reread your ten statements now to begin to internalize their power; they represent your vision for your ideal life! Return to this list whenever necessary to remind yourself why you're working so hard and to help ensure that you're making decisions that support your vision. (Suggestion: ***Mark the page in a way that will make it easily accessible; for example, put a sticky note on the page, extending slightly from the edge of your YOLO journal, or place a copy of the page where you will see it often or be able to access it quickly when needed.)***

Note: This document is a work in progress. As your ideals change, make changes to this document to reflect your new vision of your ideal life.

Your Plan

Making a dramatic life change doesn't require diving in head first. **Dramatic change results from a steady pattern of small advances, not one monumental shift.** You can and should take baby steps. It is important to pace yourself and keep your eye on the ultimate prize—your moment-to-moment happiness—so you do not run out of energy before you achieve your goals. For example, just five minutes of looking at job descriptions online might motivate you if you're thinking about changing jobs, even if you stay in your current line of work for the time being.

One important step is to make yourself accountable. Schedule regular reports on your progress with one of your friends or your life coach. This added level of commitment works wonders. Having to do what you said you would do is a powerful motivation.

Be gentle with yourself, and go easy. Like joining a gym in January of a new year, many people focus feverishly on current goals for a few months. Then day-to-day life slowly starts to interfere, the gym is abandoned, and bad feelings about another failure come to the surface. If you take small, regular steps toward your desires instead, you'll be able to maintain a steady, consistent momentum—and be successful.

A few years ago, I had a personal epiphany while addressing a large group of professionals on the subject of work–life balance.

> *I walked participants through an exercise called the Wheel of Life, which involves rating personal satisfaction in eight life areas (a shorter version of the Ten Facets of Your Ideal Life). While leading the exercise, I silently took a personal inventory, thinking about how one category was always the same: I needed to improve my health. For a long time, I had felt a black cloud of guilt materialize over my head whenever I thought about my physical self-care. So typically, after an inventory like this, I'd adopt a strict regimen of exercise and salads for two or three months before slipping back into my normal unhealthy routine until the next visit from the black cloud. It was a vicious cycle.*
>
> *Midway through that meeting, I realized that I didn't sense that black cloud over my head! Even though I had been fully prepared to berate myself out of habit, in fact I felt* ***very good*** *about my health!*
>
> *With some reflection, I realized that the black cloud had been dissipating over a few years. The process started when I borrowed* Nutrition for Dummies, *which languished on my bookshelf for six months before I began to read it. Meanwhile, one day I decided to jog instead of walk and kind of liked it. I proceeded to jog, gently, whenever I felt like it—no schedule, no pressure. I used my running time to observe the wonder of nature and to reflect on the gratitude in my life, and I really enjoyed it.*

Eventually I began to leaf through the nutrition book and was intrigued enough to take cooking lessons, which were lots of fun. I also kept jogging without a rigid schedule. Soon I started getting a massage once a month to offset stress and boost my immune system; it also felt fabulous. After about a year or so of jogging, cooking lessons and massages, I took a yoga class and found that I adored the sensation of stretching my muscles in time with my breathing.

As I recalled this slow progression of events, I discovered that my self-care habits had improved considerably. I was eating healthful food, exercising regularly and practicing several forms of stress reduction. I also weighed a few pounds less. The cloud was gone! A slow, almost imperceptible process of incremental improvements moved me toward my vision of health and vitality.

Make your journey toward your ideal life a slow-and-steady, relaxed adventure. **Keep moving forward, and consider every step—no matter the size—an achievement.** Trust that your consistency in taking small steps toward your vision will produce a wonderful result over time. It did for me, and it will for you.

Complete Exercise 25: Organize Your Action Items to impose some order on your results from Exercise 23: Develop Action Items (for Each Facet). Your results will be an easy-to-use, organized checklist that will serve as a starting point as well as a reference tool for your journey toward your ideal life.

EXERCISE 25:

Organize Your Action Items

After completing Exercises 21–23 for the Ten Facets of Your Ideal Life, you probably have thirty or more action items listed in your YOLO journal! Organize and prioritize these items to make progress along your path easier to plan and achieve.

→ To begin, refer back to the notes in your YOLO journal from earlier in this chapter.

1. Find your answers to question #2 in Exercise 23: Develop Action Items (for Each Facet) for the first facet you worked on.

2. Estimate how long it will take to complete each action item. In your YOLO journal, create four columns that reflect how long it will take to complete each action item: **one day or less, one week or less, one month or less, and more than one month.** Assign your action items to columns according to the estimated time required to complete them.

3. Replace each action item in the last column (more than one month) with several more specific action items that can be completed in one month or less. Assign these new action items to their appropriate columns.

4. Assign due dates to each action item, each of which will be achievable within one month. Schedule these dates on your calendar, with the first action item due **within the next four weeks** and the last action item due **within the next twelve months.**

5. **Repeat this exercise for each of the remaining facets of life. If you have an action item that realistically will require more than twelve months to complete, repeat this exercise annually to plan the more specific action items that will bring you closer to your goal.**

As they say, Rome was not built in a day! Taking a methodical approach to your action items will make the process manageable and help you stay motivated.

Helpful Hints

As you begin to move toward your goals, you may find yourself procrastinating or feeling woefully unprepared. Notice, I said *feeling*, not actually *being*, unprepared. Some people feel ill-equipped even after years of preparation; for others, an hour can be adequate to build the confidence needed for a new adventure. The difference is your feeling about the action you need to take.

Try breaking down the process into smaller steps. A larger task can be daunting; smaller steps are more manageable.

Speak your truth aloud. Make a list of exactly what will make you feel prepared, then share it with a friend. Saying it out loud will help you overcome any fears holding you back.

Make failure an option. Yes, you read that correctly. True happiness is about *choice*, and to successfully bring your new and improved future to life, you must be able to accept the possible failure of any incremental step along the way; you must have a backup plan. If you do not feel protected by a backup plan, you will not feel safe enough to embrace your choices freely. In this case, failure is related to meeting your own expectations for an outcome. You must clearly understand your immediate goals, not let disappointments stop your efforts and always be prepared to pursue other avenues toward your expectations.

Keep your eye on the prize (your goals), and try lots of different approaches if you need to. The means by which you eventually achieve your goals may not be what you planned for or expected at the outset. When faced with a failure, ask yourself, "What must I do to continue moving toward my vision?" and keep on moving forward.

The vision, goals and action items that you identified in Step 3: Design Your Ideal Life will serve as your road map going forward. In Step 4: Redefine What It Means to Be Productive, you will learn how to redefine *productivity* so you can manage your time effectively and move toward your ideal life.

STEP FOUR

Redefine What It Means to Be Productive

Enjoying life is not lazy or irresponsible behavior; it's just the opposite. Learn how to resist the societal pressures commonly associated with the word "productive" (both at work and at home) and discover that enjoying your life may be the most productive thing you will ever do.

The real fruition of life is to do the things we have said we wish to do.

–Woodrow Wilson

Terms Used in This Chapter

lifespan productivity: the important, constructive and beneficial value that accumulates from enjoyable and/or meaningful activities in life; a measure of overall life satisfaction

face time game: a clear and needless demonstration to oneself or to others that work takes first priority

false priorities: beliefs that make you place unwarranted importance on a situation and prevent you from taking time for lifespan-productive activities

In Step 1: Put "Enjoy Life" Back on the Agenda, you started adding more happy moments to your life and slowing down. In Step 2: Go Inward to Find Your Answers, you accessed your innate wisdom for answers to life questions. And in Step 3: Design Your Ideal Life, you clarified your ideals regarding the Ten Facets of Your Ideal Life and created goals and a plan for achieving them.

In Step 4: Redefine What It Means to Be Productive, you will begin to view your to-do list with a new perspective, so you can prioritize tasks in a way that supports your ideal life.

The Value of Time

We are traditionally rather proud of ourselves for having slipped creative work in there between the domestic chores and obligations. I'm not sure we deserve such big A-plusses for that.

-Toni Morrison

In general, most modern societies don't value the pursuit of happiness because being creative, appreciating the beauty of nature, relaxing with loved ones and simply enjoying one's good fortune are not considered legitimately productive activities. Instead, people feel compelled to keep moving, from place to place or task to task, staying busy (or appearing to do so). Yet instead of adding joy or enrichment to their lives, that constant activity only tires them out and wears them down.

Meanwhile, activities that make people happy are squeezed into schedules here and there, saved for vacations or done on the fly in between "important" to-do items, errands and obligations. As a result, people feel like they never have enough time—or control over their time—to do the things that make them happy. Even those who have a clear vision of their ideal life still feel guilty, irresponsible or even lazy taking time each day to just enjoy life.

The thing is, engaging in life-enhancing activities brings many greatly undervalued yet important benefits, such as high vitality and life satisfaction, cherished memories, good health, a sense of well-being and deep personal connections. They may also result in some of the benefits of slowing down listed in Step 1: Put "Enjoy Life" Back on the Agenda, like closer relationships, more accomplishments and consistent progress, as well as increased mental clarity, creativity, innovation and time. This aggregate value is what I call *lifespan productivity.* It's a different kind of productivity that is unique to each person and allows time for personal happiness as well as necessary responsibilities.

Lifespan-productive activities are enjoyable, meaningful or both. For example, driving a friend or relative to a doctor's appointment might feel meaningful but not enjoyable, sunning at the beach on a beautiful day might feel enjoyable but not particularly meaningful, and visiting a good friend could feel both enjoyable and meaningful. **You can recognize an activity as being lifespan-productive for you when you feel that you are exactly where you should be and doing what you want to be doing in that moment**; it just feels right.

In this chapter, you will learn how to balance lifespan productivity with work and home productivity.

> *Freelance writer, Elizabeth, expressed the concept of* lifespan productivity *perfectly when she shared her experience with me: "Working with two kids at home (most of the time) has made me incredibly disciplined with my time, but I still get frustrated when I'm busy with freelance work and can lose sight of why I left my full-time job: I wanted to be home with my kids more. Stopping and focusing on my boys gets me back on track. For instance, I played three games of Candyland this morning, and now I feel great!"*

Society's Definitions

In American society especially, the current interpretation of what kinds of activities are productive is often at odds with the goals of the You Only Live Once (YOLO) program. Whereas coasting values and encourages happy in-between moments (Step 1: Put "Enjoy Life" Back on the Agenda) and self-inquiry can bring answers to longstanding personal questions (Step 2: Go Inward to Find Your Answers), a culture in overdrive does not allow for such reflective and introspective activities. From society's perspective, if you're not moving full-speed ahead, 24/7, then you must not be busy. If you're not busy, then you must not be productive. And when it comes down to it, not being productive is simply unacceptable.

Work Productivity

The complete disconnect between the common concept of productivity and the human need to experience happiness struck me poignantly one Friday shortly after starting a leadership position at my last high-tech job.

> *Valerie, an account representative, was crying at her desk. (Our desks were only a few feet apart, so it was impossible not to notice.) Like most of my staff, she took her job seriously, but I hadn't learned much more about her.*
>
> *Not wanting to pry, I asked tentatively, "Is there anything I can do to help?"*
>
> *She said no at first, then explained, "My boyfriend is mad at me. We were supposed to go away tonight, and I just canceled." Assuming they had broken up, I nodded and remained quiet.*
>
> *"He's really angry because it's the second time I've done this," she continued. "I just can't take Saturday off; I've got too much to do here."*
>
> *Her words floored me. I had assumed that her reasons were personal. I wasn't aware of any work that would have required her attention over the weekend.*

When I asked what she needed to do, Valerie listed three routine tasks. Still puzzled, I wondered why they needed to be done on a weekend and why they were more important than plans with her boyfriend.

"Can't you do those things on Monday?" I asked. "You are always on top of your work, and it sounds like you need a break. Call your boyfriend back and go if you want to."

Sounding both relieved and surprised, she thanked me, picked up the phone and dialed at the speed of light, perhaps afraid I might change my mind.

I was happy to support Valerie in balancing her work and personal lives because, to me, it was part of being a good leader. However, I suspected this incident wasn't an isolated one. Asking around, I discovered that Valerie routinely worked twelve- to thirteen-hour days, six or seven days a week. I couldn't understand the need to work so many hours in the absence of emergencies and crucial deadlines, but in fact, everyone at this company kept such a schedule. The entire organization seemed to work in fear of not appearing to be busy enough.

As it turned out, "business as usual" at this company meant a deliberately cultivated culture of what I call the *face time game.* The leadership required all employees to constantly demonstrate that work came first in their lives. It was a condition of their continued employment. Anyone who gave less risked being considered a disloyal nine-to-fiver (say it isn't so!). Even if an employee did exceptional work in an efficient way, leaving after eight or nine hours was considered slacking off and drew criticism. As a result, employees routinely sacrificed their personal lives to keep the bosses happy (and therefore keep their jobs). I quickly recognized that this company's ethos was not going to fit well with mine.

Valerie took her weekend off. The next week, I asked my boss, Jack (also the company owner), why these extra-long days and weekend hours were required. "We are a start-up," he replied simply. "It's what it takes." Even though I had worked for several other successful start-up companies and knew it not to be the only way, I worked long shifts along with everyone else, trying to figure out how to change the situation. An unexpected, harsh event—which turned out to be a blessing in disguise—solved the problem for me.

Jack called me into his office and said, "This isn't working out."

"What isn't working out?" I asked, thinking about the various projects I had recently been assigned.

"You," he said flat out. "Your working here is what's not working out." He explained that I was being fired for taking two key employees out for short one-on-one lunch meetings the previous week. "We do not leave our desks for lunch."

Flabbergasted, I tried to explain how effective the meetings had been, the legal implications of such a policy, and the many management studies showing that employees are more productive after a break, but he didn't want to hear any of it. "I have been eating lunch at my desk for thirteen years," he announced, "and that is how we do it here."

I had never been fired before. Shocked and embarrassed, I packed up and left immediately. At home, I plopped down on my couch in disbelief, self-doubt and confusion, wondering, "What just happened to me? Am I out of touch? Is this what new companies have to do to succeed these days?"

Before I could ponder these questions further, my cell phone began to ring. One by one, my former staff were going out to the parking lot and calling me from the privacy of their cars. The frantic, worried questions came fast and furious:

- *"What am I going to do now? It was awful before you worked here. Now it will be worse again."*
- *"I just started to get my life back. Now that's over. Should I stay? Should I leave?"*
- *"Are other companies any different?"*
- *"Am I qualified to work anywhere else?"*
- *"What should I do?"*

I gave advice as best I could while asking myself all the same questions.

Most people have put in a few extra hours at work *occasionally* to meet deadlines, make some overtime pay or show support for colleagues. However, when company leaders ignore the concept of lifespan productivity, they create a pressure-cooker work environment in which employees lose sight of it as well. A situation in which people are forced to make work supersede everything else in life is unnecessary and ultimately unsustainable.

Work productivity can be out of balance in other ways besides the face time game. For example, many people also forgo their lifespan productivity by not taking earned vacations; taking portable work devices *with them* on vacation; going in to work when they are ill and should stay home to recover; working with overbearing, disrespectful or verbally abusive superiors or coworkers; working in poor or unsafe conditions; being grossly underpaid for the work they do; or working full time without standard benefits. All of these situations compromise one's ability to live a happy, stable life including opportunities to enjoy well-deserved lifespan productivity.

If your typical workday is longer than you'd like, saps your energy or does not allow for important activities (like breaks), take a tip from me: Get your nose off that grindstone! Remember what makes you feel happy, grateful or energized, and find a way to do that instead once in a while.

By the way, stay-at-home parents and people with home offices: Don't be fooled. You, too, can get pulled into the face time game and deny yourself enjoyable and/or meaningful activities. If you find yourself pushing to get just one more thing done—another load of laundry, one more email or another work task—instead of making time for a game with the kids, a phone call to a friend, or a much-needed break with a book, magazine or hobby—then it's time to reevaluate.

Complete Exercise 26: Examine Your Work Productivity to challenge your perceptions about work habits so you can make choices that support consistent progress toward your ideal life.

> If you are a manager and want more information about the relationship between work productivity and lifespan productivity, consider these findings from the *Harvard Business Review* (and go to the source to read more):
>
> "Our research over the past four years in several North American offices of the Boston Consulting Group (BCG) … found that when the assumption that everyone needs to be always available was collectively challenged, not only could individuals take time off, but their work actually benefited. Our experiments with time off resulted in more open dialogue among team members, which is valuable in itself. But the improved communication also sparked new processes that enhanced the teams' ability to work most efficiently and effectively."[30]

30. Perlow, Leslie A., and Jessica L. Porter. 2009. *Making Time Off Predictable—and Required.* Harvard Business Review, Vol. 87, No. 10, pp. 102–109.

EXERCISE 26:

Examine Your Work Productivity

An important step in changing your ideas about productivity is to take stock of how your work habits affect your lifespan productivity.

→ In your YOLO journal, answer the following questions as accurately as possible.

1. How many hours do I spend working each day? Each week? *(Include commute time and weekends, if appropriate. If you work from home, do not guess or approximate this number; add up the actual hours. If you don't usually write down your hours, keep track of your hours worked for one week.)*

2. Am I required to work more hours than I would like to? If so, why? Do I agree with this requirement? Is it a temporary or permanent situation?

3. Do my work deadlines or requirements influence the choices I make in my personal life? If so, how often? Occasionally? Regularly? Often?

4. Can I (and do I) take breaks (for lunch and throughout the work period) away from my usual workspace? If so, for how long, and are they enjoyable?

5. How do I usually feel while at work? Bored? Energized? Appreciated? Challenged? Frazzled?

6. How do I feel at the end of a workday? Proud of completing a good day's work? Physically exhausted? Emotionally drained? Full of ideas for the next day?

Next, share your answers with a partner, roommate, close colleague or friend who lives with you or sees you daily. Ask them whether they believe your answers to be accurate, and if not, revisit the relevant questions until you find your most honest answers.

Finally, think about how to integrate rejuvenating breaks and coasting moments into your workday. For any of your answers to questions #2 through #6 that you would like to change, plan how to adjust your work schedule and responsibilities so you have enough energy for lifespan-productive activities.

Home Productivity

If busy-ness is a societal pandemic (see Step 1: Put "Enjoy Life" Back on the Agenda), then the lack of lifespan productivity is a societal deficiency. The normal amount of time and energy required for balanced work productivity is only one piece of the puzzle. Even in their free time, people find it challenging to put enjoyable and/or meaningful life-enriching activities first. Sadly, lifespan productivity can be *even more challenging* to achieve after hours, when faced with family and community obligations and household duties.

Let's do some math: Consider the average Monday-to-Friday work week. The typical person hopes to get eight hours of sleep at night and works eight or nine hours per workday, leaving seven or eight hours for everything else. Subtracting a conservative two hours for getting ready for work and commuting to work leaves five to six hours. Feeding oneself and perhaps family members breakfast (often a luxury nowadays), lunch and dinner takes away another two hours or so, assuming grocery shopping was done on another day. Preparing for the next day and going to sleep takes at least another hour. On a good day, what's left is a grand total of two hours to take care of personal needs, to-do items and unexpected tasks; attend evening events; and unwind in preparation for repeating it all the next day. And this estimation assumes a best-case scenario in which everything goes as planned (no traffic, tantrums or burned dinner!).

It's no wonder people never seem to have enough time during the week to do the things they want to do. That's what weekends are for, right? In theory, maybe. In reality, most people spend at least half of the weekend playing catch-up—doing the routine tasks that they didn't get to or started but didn't finish during the week, like doing laundry, paying bills and going grocery shopping—and the other half fulfilling social, community and family obligations, like making cookies for a bake sale, organizing a church dinner or attending a relative's 50th wedding anniversary shindig. What's more, a typical weekend is so jam-packed with immediate concerns that it can't accommodate longer-term tasks (e.g., household maintenance or repair projects) that have been put off repeatedly, waiting for the right moment. Making time to do something you *want* to do is not easy when faced with so many tasks that you think you *must* do.

Complete Exercise 27: Examine Your Home Productivity to challenge your perception of which personal items are required and which are optional, so you make choices that support consistent progress toward your ideal life.

EXERCISE 27:

Examine Your Home Productivity

Another important step in changing your ideas about productivity is to take stock of how the ways you choose to spend your time at home (i.e., outside of work) affect your lifespan productivity.

→ In your YOLO journal, answer the following questions as completely and accurately as you can.

1. **How often is my free time overrun by plans, to-dos and other obligations? Never? Occasionally? Regularly? Often?**
2. **How often do I regret agreeing to outside obligations because they take up too much of my free time? Never? Occasionally? Regularly? Often? If ever, for which obligations? (Note: If your answer is "often," it is time for you to rethink this commitment.)**
3. **Does my partner, child or pet suffer as a result of my unavailability for enjoyable and/or meaningful activities on weeknights or weekends?**
4. **Do I participate in enjoyable and/or meaningful activities just for me? Each day? Week? Month? If so, what are they?**
5. **When was the last time I participated in a free-time activity that made me happy?**

Next, reread your answers about life-enriching activities from Exercise 4: Identify What Has Been Missing (page 41) and Exercise 5: Enjoy Life, Today (page 46) in Step 1: Put "Enjoy Life" Back on the Agenda.

Finally, keeping in mind your answers to this exercise, think about how to incorporate activities that make you happy into your home life. Plan how you will adjust your personal obligations, volunteer commitments and sense of urgency around routine and household tasks. You may wish to use some of your newly freed-up time for life-enriching activities from your results to Exercise 25: Organize Your Action Items.

A Unique Definition

Because society's limited concept of productivity is so pervasive, most people consider enjoyable and/or meaningful activities unproductive and associate unpleasant, difficult tasks with accomplishment. How often have you said (or heard someone else say), "I spent three hours connecting with someone I love today, and I feel terrific" or "I had so much fun working on a project with my friend; I'm so proud of myself"? People need to make a habit of patting themselves on the back for taking the time to do things that are lifespan productive, like enjoying a beautiful day, lounging in a hot bath, reading a good book, or connecting with a friend. **To some people, lifespan productivity feels like irresponsibility. To a person living the life they want, lifespan productivity feels like achievement.**

Take a moment to think about your life. What do you remember—the endless hours spent getting things done or the joyful experiences you had? Your answer should help you decide which activities to prioritize, or at least get on your radar screen, going forward. And as you reprioritize, remind yourself to **feel good about choosing lifespan-productive activities.** You deserve to live a life of enjoyment, connection and vitality.

Make no mistake; it takes effort to support your lifespan productivity and create time for the enjoyable and/or meaningful activities that bring you happiness, joy and peace. It requires consistent awareness, and it's easy to fall back into old habits and miss important opportunities to experience happiness. I know, because it has happened to me.

> *My golden retriever, Sheppie, underwent major bilateral hip surgery when she was eleven months old. For weeks afterward, she needed help to stand up, walk, and even shift positions. My husband and I took turns helping her during her painful recovery.*
>
> *During one of my nursing shifts, I realized that I had been busily working the whole time and had not spent any time comforting her or paying attention to her. Even though I was physically in the room, my focus was on my work, not on Sheppie. My inner sage reminded me that consoling my dog was important because I felt sad about her pain, and this was one way I could help. I put the laptop aside and got down on the floor with my loyal friend for a while.*
>
> *Because my shift was during work hours, I had unwittingly fallen into the trap of multitasking, thinking that being productive in that moment meant paying more attention to my business than to the living, breathing being in the room with me. Although continuing to work might have been the more productive choice according to society's perspective, in the context of my life, cheering my injured pup increased my sense of well-being, connection and love. Thanks to the nudging of my inner sage, I didn't miss out on those meaningful moments.*

Your vision of your ideal life will provide the context you need to make wise decisions about how you spend your time—that is, it will help you determine whether activities are lifespan productive for you. As this awareness becomes a regular part of your decision-making process, you will recognize the unique and fundamental value of making time for key activities that feed your soul.

Until you define, embrace and live your own definition of *lifespan productivity,* you will be unable to compete with the pressures of what society customarily considers productive; you just won't be able to feel good about spending time on activities that simply enrich your life. To redefine your understanding of (and get a new perspective on) *productivity*, complete Exercise 28: Define Your Lifespan Productivity. Your true priorities will come into clear focus, and you will be able to allot time to your goals from Step 3: Design Your Ideal Life and be happier as a result. Then, complete Exercise 29: Is This Activity Lifespan Productive? to quickly determine whether an activity supports your vision of your ideal life.

EXERCISE 28:

Define Your Lifespan Productivity

The *American Heritage Dictionary* defines the word productive as "yielding favorable or useful results." This meaning has changed dramatically in common usage; productivity is more likely to be associated with work and obligation than with play and pleasure. However, most people can name a wide range of activities that yield "favorable or useful results" over their lifetimes, particularly in the context of their own happiness.

→ In your YOLO journal, look back to your answers from Exercise 24: Clarify Your Vision in Step 3: Design Your Ideal Life. Think about the activities that contribute to your overall life satisfaction—that is, the activities that are valuable and lifespan productive for you and help you move toward your vision of your ideal life. Ask yourself,

1. Which activities enrich my life and are enjoyable and/or meaningful?
2. Which activities are most likely to "yield useful or favorable results" toward living my ideal life?

After you have reflected for a few moments, write down two or three sentences to describe what lifespan productivity means to you in your YOLO journal. For example:

- "Playing with my kids is lots of fun and reminds me how lucky I am to be a parent."
- "Taking 30 minutes for myself every day gives me quiet time to recharge and appreciate my life."
- "Spending a few hours with a good friend makes me happy because I feel valued and connected."

Use this awareness to make sure you put these elements on your daily to-do list.

EXERCISE 29:

Is This Activity Lifespan Productive?

You may occasionally find yourself in an activity (or situation) that doesn't feel like a good use of your time; even though you are here, you wish you were there. You must be able to first recognize that the activity does not promote your well-being and then determine how to choose a lifespan-productive one instead.

→ To learn how to judge whether an activity is lifespan productive for you, think back to a time when you found yourself doing one thing but wishing you could be doing another—perhaps you were stuck in a late meeting on a weeknight, toiling in your yard on a hot day or running endless errands on a weekend afternoon. Something about the activity just didn't make you happy, but you might not have been able to put your finger on the reason.

Imagine that you're still in the activity for a moment, and consult your inner sage. Ask yourself,

1. Why do I feel uncomfortable?
2. Can I make this activity meaningful, enjoyable and lifespan productive?
3. Would I like to become more engaged by changing my role? If so, how?
4. If I would rather disengage, where would I rather be? What would I rather be doing?

Your inner sage won't lie. It will tell you your true priorities. Perhaps you do not value the activity, so your time would be better spent elsewhere. Maybe the activity is valuable and lifespan productive, but you need to adjust your focus and involvement in the moment to reconnect to why you have chosen to be there.

Whenever you find yourself feeling trapped in a situation, repeat this exercise to determine whether the activity contributes to your lifespan productivity. If it does not, make the appropriate changes to make it so.

Your Own Path

People with goals succeed because they know where they're going.

-Earl Nightingale

By and large, most people feel guilty spending free time enjoying themselves when they could be productive (what they really mean is busy) instead. But in reality, because happiness creates vitality, nothing could be more productive than taking opportunities for enjoyable activities. Each person's path to an ideal life is paved with the lifespan-productive choices they make every day.

My experience with Valerie and other co-workers at that high-tech start-up changed me forever. I no longer wanted to contribute to work environments where personal lives were not only severely undervalued but also explicitly discouraged. In an odd twist of fate, my dismissal from that job solidified the importance of standing up for lifespan productivity—both my own and that of my former staff.

My first step after being fired was to get in touch with Mike, the life coach from my previous job who had asked me the tough questions about what I wanted to do with my life. When I told him that I was starting to lean toward life coaching myself, he put me in touch with several colleagues to research training programs. I ultimately enrolled in the two-year program at Coach University and simultaneously opened my doors as a "coach in training." It was a tough two years of trying to make ends meet, pay tuition, attend classes and earn a minuscule income as a trainee, but I was motivated because coaching offered me the best of both worlds. I could honor my own definition of lifespan productivity while having the privilege of showing others how to do the same.

After coaching for a while, I was intrigued to discover that even as a self-employed life coach, I was haunted by old notions of productivity. Fighting the urge to measure my output by hours spent at my desk, number of emails answered or how immaculate my house was, I continually reminded myself to stay focused on my definition of *lifespan* productivity. Of course, external reminders were helpful, too!

> *Shortly after I started my coaching business, my friend Kevin called. At the time, he was a successful senior manager at a large company that had been growing rapidly. He and his team had been working long hours and traveling often. He was also married with four children, all under the age of ten.*
>
> *As we caught up on each other's lives, I commented that he talked about teaching his five-year-old daughter to ice skate and coaching his nine-year-old son's hockey games just as often as his meetings and business trips. His response? "Well, you gotta remember what really matters."*

Kevin had a clear picture of his ideal life and put it into practice every day by choosing activities that were lifespan productive.

Honoring your lifespan productivity requires *awareness* coupled with *prioritization.* Because you created a clear vision of your ideal life in Step 3: Design Your Ideal Life, you are aware of what makes your life rich. With that knowledge it is now possible, and necessary, to give priority to the activities that promote and protect your new life.

If you ever feel guilty that you're neglecting your professional or personal responsibilities in favor of lifespan-productive activities, take out your YOLO journal and review your answers to Exercise 28: Define Your Lifespan Productivity. Then ask yourself, "Would my extra time have really been better spent doing whatever I was feeling guilty about?" Chances are, no amount of additional hours spent increasing your work or home productivity could match the deep satisfaction that you gained from choosing to be lifespan productive—doing things that you enjoy and that enrich your life. I rarely, if ever, look back and regret having spent time relaxing, making a connection with someone, being creative or simply enjoying a moment in life. Give yourself permission to live the life you want! Remember, the happier you are, the more you can contribute to the world by sharing your energy, creativity and enthusiasm for life. Imagine what the world would be like if every person were more energetic and innovative!

One important area in which people tend to lose sight of lifespan productivity is routine obligations—usually volunteer activities that used to be important but aren't any longer—that they thought would be fun but turned out not to be, or that they had a difficult time saying no to originally. Complete Exercise 30: Are My Obligations Lifespan Productive? to determine whether your routine obligations support your vision of your ideal life.

EXERCISE 30:

Are My Obligations Lifespan Productive?

Becoming aware of whether recurring activities are lifespan productive for you will help you stay on track toward your goals and the life you want. Evaluate and take a critical look at your routine obligations, then eliminate those that are not lifespan productive.

→ Take a moment to consider your routine obligations—for example, volunteer endeavors, community responsibilities, group memberships and other personal commitments. Look at your calendar, and list such commitments for the next month in your YOLO journal.

Next, in your YOLO journal, answer the following questions about each obligation:

1. **What about this obligation do I enjoy the most?**
2. **Do I feel resentful or as if I am wasting my time?** ***(These feelings are an indication that the activity is not lifespan productive for you.)***
3. **Why did I originally become involved?**
4. **Why am I still doing it? Because I genuinely want to? To look good? Because I am afraid to say no?**
5. **Which (whose) definition of productivity am I following?**
6. **Would I feel more happy, connected or energized about this obligation if something were different?**
7. **What specific changes would make this activity lifespan productive?** ***(List as many changes as would have to occur for this to happen.)***
8. **What would happen if I were no longer associated with this obligation?**

From your answers to questions #1–8, choose to continue this obligation with any necessary adaptations (the answers to question #7), or take steps to eliminate it from your routine. Then ask yourself,

9. **How should I approach similar obligations in the future?**

Repeat this exercise for each of your listed routine obligations. Come back to this exercise whenever you question whether an obligation is on track toward your vision of your ideal life.

New Life, New Habits

Planning is bringing the future into the present so that you can do something about it now.

-Alan Lakein

Because lifespan productivity involves consistent progress toward overall life satisfaction, it can be helpful to create supportive rituals or traditions. As the rituals and traditions become habit, making lifespan-productive decisions will become more natural and eventually automatic.

Bernard-Paul Heroux, a philosopher from the early 1900s, said, "There is no trouble so great or grave that cannot be much diminished by a nice cup of tea." I couldn't agree more. In fact, one of my oldest friendships grew out of a simple tradition and self-created ritual: drinking tea, and lots of it.

> *Over the years, Deborah and I have sat around all manner of tables drinking pots of tea while talking over the important and not-so-important issues in our lives. We share mundane details about hair styles and explore deeply emotional life questions in the same conversation, then laugh about it.*
>
> *Deborah and I met when we were ten and twelve years old, respectively. We grew up together, seeing each other through the milestones of adolescence, college and adulthood. Today, when we need to connect, one of us simply says that we need to "sit down and have some tea"—even when our connection is by phone, across thousands of miles.*

I constantly remind myself to make time for my friends and family because those closest connections bring me joy. Enjoying and nurturing key relationships is as lifespan productive to me as any other pursuit, if not more so.

What kinds of regular, prearranged activities make you feel happy or fulfilled? You may already have some lifespan-productive rituals or traditions. Some examples from my clients include:

- Reading to or with their kids before bed each night
- Shopping at a weekly farmers' market
- Taking a nature walk on the same day each month
- Hosting a potluck dinner seasonally
- Seeing new blockbuster movies with a best friend on opening night
- Taking a painting class each year

The activities you enjoy should be regular, not rare and haphazard. **The beauty of any ritual or tradition is that it is uncomplicated, unique to you and purposeful;** that time is scheduled and dedicated to a pursuit that makes your life worth living.

Create some new habits to increase your sense of well-being, and you'll soon see how happy these activities make you feel. To take your first steps, complete Exercise 31: Start Something New and choose an activity that is lifespan productive for you.

EXERCISE 31:

Start Something New

To increase your lifespan productivity, you must prioritize the activities that are meaningful and enjoyable.

→ Think about some activities that make you happy. What would you like to do regularly but currently do not? Meditate? Walk with a friend? Engage in a fun project with your child? The timing is irrelevant. It could be a one-minute grace tradition before each meal, a fifteen-minute journaling ritual each morning or a one-hour piano practice once a week.

Pick one new ritual and schedule it on your calendar right now. Then ask a supportive friend, family member or housemate to check in with you in two weeks to see how it's going. Planning and consistency are the keys to your success.

Incorporating a new tradition or ritual that reinforces your definition of *lifespan productivity* may require changing your normal routine—for example, watching less television or letting household chores wait one more day—but the results will be worth it because your choices will be directly in line with your vision of your ideal life.

Helpful Hints

When you're making dramatic life changes, it's easy to be derailed by *false priorities*, that is, beliefs that make you place unwarranted importance on a situation and prevent you from being lifespan productive. They can momentarily blind you and stop you from moving toward your vision of your ideal life.

Recognize false priorities! You will know when you are struggling with one when you feel torn, unsettled or ambivalent about your commitment to someone or something. The five most common false priorities I hear from my clients and the likely underlying causes of each follow:

"I must look good to [fill in the blank]."	Pride
"I need more time."	Perfectionism or procrastination
"I'm stuck in my situation and can't change it."	Lack of self-confidence
"I am needed by these people or this organization (even though they do not enrich my life)."	Insecurity
"I have to be judged as productive by [fill in the blank]."	Unclear definition of your own lifespan productivity

Remind yourself what matters most. To regain your clarity and release yourself from a false priority, reread your answers to Exercise 21: Describe Your Ideal (for Each Facet) from Step 3: Design Your Ideal Life for the facet(s) most closely related to your situation. By recognizing that a false priority is holding you back, you should be able to question its validity, address its cause and move forward. If you can't figure out how to do that on your own, seek advice from a partner, friend or life coach.

When you are clinging to a false priority, understanding your personal definition of lifespan productivity will help. You will sense when things are not right, be more aware of how you spend your time and be able to progress toward your vision of your ideal. To learn how to maintain your lifespan productivity even when you think you can't, continue to Step 5: Build Your Self-Confidence.

Build Your Self-Confidence

CREATING YOUR NEW LIFE REQUIRES TAKING THE REINS AND BREAKING AWAY FROM UNNECESSARY RULES THAT LIMIT YOUR OPTIONS. LEARN HOW TO EMBRACE YOUR POWER, RECOGNIZE AND OVERCOME OBSTACLES, AND MAKE WISE DECISIONS SO YOU CAN BE IN CONTROL OF YOUR DESTINY—EVEN WHEN YOU THINK YOU CAN'T.

Whatever you can do, or dream you can do, begin it. Boldness has a genius, power, and magic in it.

~GOETHE

Terms Used in This Chapter

creative confidence: trust in one's ability to try new approaches

limited thinking: unnecessary rules about how something must be done, with the belief that no other alternative exists; the absence of creative confidence

So far in the You Only Live Once (YOLO) program, you have been challenged to do lots of self-observation of your lifestyle, your innermost needs, your vision of an ideal life and your own definition of *lifespan productivity.* As you put these concepts into action, you have been slowing down, coasting, consulting your inner sage, defining your personal goals and creating action items to achieve those goals.

In Step 5: Build Your Self-Confidence you will learn how to feel strong and self-assured by creating a network of people who support you and your efforts, freeing yourself from self-defeating thoughts by tapping in to your creativity, and taking the risks required to design and achieve your ideal life. Your desire to live a life you love—combined with a clear vision of your ideal life—will empower you to be innovative in making it a reality.

A Web of Support

Perfect as the wing of a bird may be, it will never enable the bird to fly if unsupported by the air.

-Ivan Pavlov

Contrary to popular belief, redesigning a life is not a solitary pursuit. Striving toward an ever-evolving vision is challenging, and having support available will go a long way in boosting your confidence and your chances for success. Building the life you want requires creating a network of people who can help you out from time to time. "Help" might mean a babysitter to create space for coasting, expert advice to provide direction or a friendly ear to brainstorm ideas and alternatives. Different people and groups provide different kinds of support, but all are important elements.

People You Know

At some point while you are putting the YOLO program into practice, you will need to ask for help. The obvious first place to look is to the people who are closest to you: family and friends. You may have approached many of them already while working through previous steps of the YOLO program, in which case you have an idea what they think of your plans. These people generally have your best interests at heart and are supportive of your progress.

Of course, not everyone who is important to you will be supportive of this "design an ideal life" stuff. In fact, some may be downright negative or openly in opposition to your choices. But you might need to ask them for help anyway.

Complete Exercise 32: Ask for Support to learn how to ask people you know for the help you need to achieve your goals.

EXERCISE 32:
Ask for Support

You probably have an idea who among your nearest and dearest will be and will not be supportive of your decisions before you ask for help. The preparation for a meeting with either kind of person is the same.

⟶ Schedule a convenient time (for both of you) to have a relaxed conversation. Before your meeting, take time to clarify your needs. In your YOLO journal, write down how, specifically, this person can help you create your ideal life. The help you need might be general (e.g., talking through your action items, providing money to fund an endeavor or checking in with you periodically to make sure that your progress is on track) or specific (e.g., purchasing or lending you a map or a portable navigation device if you wish to travel, or helping you rearrange your living space to make it feel more homey to you).

Be as precise and as clear as you can. It is best to ask for help that is as well-defined as possible, action-oriented and limited in scope. For instance, you might ask, "Because you know so much about art, would you accompany me to the art store to help me select the proper materials for oil painting?" instead of "Will you be supportive of me in my desire to become an artist?"

After making this list of needs, write down who else might assist you with these needs if the first person you ask is unable or unwilling to help you.

If you want to request help from someone who is supportive of your life changes:

1. Share your vision of your ideal life to demonstrate your passion, motivation and commitment. *(Always start with this step, even if they have heard your vision before! Doing so will start the conversation on a positive note.)*

2. Explain why their support is important to you and how it is different from the support of others.

3. From the list in your YOLO journal, state one or two ways that they can help you. *(Start with the most essential; you can always ask for help again later. If you ask for too many things right away, the conversation can become muddled and overwhelming.)*

4. Courteously work out the specifics (i.e., when, where and how they will help you) and schedule mutually convenient appointments, if necessary.

5. Thank them for their support.

If you want to request help from someone whose support you want but aren't currently getting:

1. Share your vision of your ideal life to demonstrate your passion, motivation and commitment. *(Always start with this step, even if they have heard your vision before! Doing so will start the conversation on a positive note.)*

2. Explain why their support is important to you and how it is different from the support of others.

3. Ask whether they have any fears related to your plans. If so, be sure to let them fully explain how they feel without interruption; do not dismiss them! *(Fears are most effectively released only after they have been completely expressed. Remember that this person likes you, so any hesitation on their part probably comes from a feeling of fear for your well-being. By openly discussing these fears, you can dispel them together.)*

4. Ask for their confidence; ask them to trust that you know what you are doing and that you will seek help if you need it. (They may not realize that their own fears and corresponding lack of support imply a lack of confidence in your ability to manage your life and solve problems creatively.)

5. From the list in your YOLO journal, state one or two ways in which they can help you. *(Start with the most essential; you can always ask for help again later. If you ask for too many things right away, the conversation can become muddled and overwhelming.)*

6. If they agree to support you in some way, courteously work out the specifics (i.e., when, where and how they will help you), schedule mutually convenient appointments, if necessary, and thank them for their offer. If they don't, just thank them for listening.

If this person has refused to help you after you have followed all six steps, then seek assistance elsewhere. This person might change their mind after you begin to show signs of success, which will allay their fears, but until then, go your own way without them.

Return to your YOLO journal, consult the list you created of other people you could to turn to for help with this issue and try this same process with them.

If you know what you need but don't know a person who can help you with it, it's time to start networking! Make a list of your most ardent supporters. Might any of them have contacts in the area you need help with? Following the instructions above, ask them whether they would be willing to introduce you to someone who could provide an informational interview, suggest contacts who might be able to mentor you or provide relevant resources (e.g., websites and organizations).

No matter what your situation, keep track of your best supporters in your YOLO journal. Refer back to this list later so you can send thank-you notes or other tokens when you are fully enjoying your new life. It's always nice to remember who helped you get to where you want to be!

People You Don't Know—Yet!

Friends and family make up a rather limited group. Growing a support network requires making contact with people outside of this immediate circle. New acquaintances and friends of friends fall into this category, but keep the focus on connecting with people who have similar interests or are taking positive life-changing steps themselves.

Folks who are taking action to improve their lives have the same mind-set as you and know what it's like to overcome obstacles. They have great potential to be creative and helpful because, like you, they are in a place of growth and are not afraid of change. They also are likely to welcome the opportunity for mutual support.

Good places to meet such people include classes, special events and social interest groups—a night course about starting a business, a YOLO seminar, a running group training for a charity marathon, a professional mastermind group, a social networking association, a personal coaching group that meets (in person or via telephone) to track each other's progress, or even online forums. You also could create or join a local YOLO support group (learn how on my website, www.youonlyliveoncebook.com), a terrific way to get support in person.

Many groups can be found by searching the Internet. For example, local colleges, community recreation departments and continuing education programs usually post class listings online. Online newspapers post weekly calendars of activities for local organizations. Meetup (www.meetup.com) allows users to search for local groups by interest and ZIP code. Yahoo! Groups (groups.yahoo.com) and Google Groups (groups.google.com) host innumerable online discussion groups organized by common interest. (**Note:** All of these resources are also listed in Online Resources on page 227.) Online forums, websites and topical blogs offer opportunities to interact with like-minded folks all over the world whenever you have time to be online.

Confidence and Creativity

There are two primary choices in life: to accept conditions as they exist, or to accept the responsibility for changing them.

–Denis Waitley

The journey toward an ideal life is not necessarily smooth sailing the entire way. It's completely expected and normal to sometimes feel stuck, without options, afraid or hesitant. Making change is one of the most difficult things a person can do, and the subconscious mind may balk at challenges to the status quo!

As you continue to move toward your goals, you will inevitably face opposition from inside yourself. To confront and ultimately overcome such road blocks, you must recognize them, access your innate creativity to come up with alternative courses of action and then keep moving toward your ideal life. Once you begin to recognize that such obstacles exist, you will be prepared to overcome them with confidence.

A Stuck Mind-Set

A person's ability to come up with innovative solutions may be restricted by concerns about why things might not work because of potential, perceived or existing obstacles. I call unnecessary fear-based rules that people create for themselves *limited thinking*. This kind of mind-set is often reflected in "I" beliefs (e.g., "I have to …" "I'm the only one who can …" and "I must …") or feelings of being overwhelmed that lead to inaction. Everyone is susceptible to limited thinking.

When fear really takes hold, it can be overpowering, making rational and creative thinking difficult and all but destroying self-confidence. Some examples of fearful, limited thinking are:

- I have to stay in this job I hate because I'm lucky to have a job at all.

- My relationship no longer supports me, but I stay because I don't know if I'll ever find a better one.

- My lifestyle leaves no time for myself or the things that I like to do, but I have no way to change my circumstances.

You might believe that there is only one way to reach your goal, whether it's a place, a position or a state of being; however, alternatives always exist. The issue is seeing them, which may require some intervention.

When I sat down to write this chapter, I followed my normal new-chapter writing procedure: I wrote emails, had a snack, cleared my desktop of random projects, had lunch, and then—at about two-thirty in the afternoon, with nothing left to distract me—was ready to start writing. I opened my file drawer for the thick folder of notes, articles and quotes labeled Step 5. I saw Steps 1 through 4, but where was Step 5?

In a panic, I scoured the drawer, my office and my car, worried that I had lost the material needed to write this chapter. My fruitless search left me feeling frustrated, discouraged and devoid of all creativity—not to mention a little annoyed with myself. For days, I was unable to write because I needed my notes, and berated myself with thoughts like, "What kind of so-called author loses a whole chapter file?" and "What makes me think I can write this book at all?" I was ready to pack in the whole darn project.

A few days after I lost my Step 5 notes—still not writing—I had a coaching call with my colleague Claudette. I told her that I had lost at least two years' worth of notes and how it had soured my feelings toward the entire book project.

"I know how aggravating it is to lose something essential like that," she empathized. "What is the chapter about?" Claudette asked.

> *"It's about breaking out of situations that are holding you back and accessing your power of innovation to move forward in new ways. It's about realizing that you are ultimately in control and have the skills you need to shape your life the way you want it."*
>
> *"That sounds great. Couldn't losing this file be considered a situation that's holding you back and an opportunity to create a new way of writing?"*
>
> *"Wow," I laughed, impressed with her (obvious, I now realize) observation. "I have been creating unnecessary rules about the process, believing there was no other way. Of course I* ***can*** *write this chapter! It will be different, and possibly more difficult to write this way, but I'm sure once I get going, I will remember ninety-nine percent of my notes."*

I had come face-to-face with the very demon I planned to warn you about! When I was stuck in my limited thinking, fear took hold and created doubts about the whole project, including the chapters that were already done. I felt incompetent to write, with or without notes. Perhaps it was destiny. (And no, I never did find that file folder.)

When you feel stuck and have no options, look for an alternative—even if you are absolutely convinced that none exists. To get beyond limited thinking, you must shift your brain out of one-way thinking by gaining a new or broader perspective, usually with the help of another person. You can do this by talking through the situation with one of your supporters (as I did with Claudette).

An even better way to thoroughly break out of limited thinking is to bombard yourself with as many alternate ideas or approaches as you can come up with. Brainstorming is a technique for maximizing creative thinking, and it can be used to solve a problem (e.g., a lost file), overcome an obstacle (e.g., a lack of money) or generate a new approach to a situation (e.g., how to finish a project on time). A short exercise can break you out of the limited thinking box. Complete Exercise 33: Brainstorm Past Limited Thinking to free your mind so you can explore new possibilities.

EXERCISE 33:

Brainstorm Past Limited Thinking

Think about a current problem or an area in which you are feeling stuck, and prepare yourself to come up with all sorts of possible solutions. You can work alone, but working with one or more supportive people will make the exercise more effective. For that reason, this exercise assumes that you will work with others. It is particularly helpful (but not necessary) to include people who have experience or knowledge in the area in which you need help.

→ To begin, meet in a private, relaxed location where you can speak aloud and be free from interruptions for about 30 minutes. Have plenty of note paper available, and make sure that everyone can see the master list by using a large sheet of paper, a whiteboard or a chalkboard.

1. Explain the brainstorming guidelines to everyone present:
    - Speak clearly, so everyone can hear the ideas.
    - Say whatever comes to mind! Don't stifle an idea that seems unrealistic, impossible or even silly. Share it anyway. ALL ideas are encouraged. *(You will worry about practicality later. Besides, I have seen some remarkable, very workable ideas emerge from silly or unrealistic beginnings!)*
    - No negative judgments are allowed about anyone's ideas!

2. Ask a volunteer to take notes on the master list. *(It is best if someone else is the note-taker so you can be free to keep thinking of ideas.)*

3. Share your vision of your ideal outcome to demonstrate your passion, motivation and commitment.

4. Explain how your current problem (about which you feel stuck) is thwarting your efforts to move toward your goals (e.g., "I want to start a new business selling cookies, but I have a tiny kitchen").

5. Ask a specific question that will begin to generate answers to help solve your problem (e.g., "How can I access a kitchen big enough to bake cookies for my business?"). Be honest, clear and fact-oriented.

6. List *all the suggested ideas* on the master list. After everyone has run out of ideas, review the list together and select the best, most realistic solutions to your problem.

7. For each possible solution, brainstorm your next steps for either gathering more information or putting the idea into action.

8. Thank everyone for their participation.

Repeat this exercise whenever you feel stuck on one of your YOLO goals or frustrated in any other situation. Remember that you can do this exercise on your own, too, if needed. However, if you do, be mindful not to self-censor your ideas!

Trusting Yourself

Imagine driving on a highway and coming upon a traffic jam. A string of red taillights is stretched out for miles ahead. You have a choice: Stay on your current course and wait for the traffic to clear, or turn off at the next available exit and try to find an alternate route to your destination. Most likely, you will attempt another route only if you are confident in your ability to find your way along the new road. This confidence comes from within. You trust that you will be able to find your way by using a combination of your instinct, navigational tools, knowledge of the area and willingness to ask for help.

Life can be challenging, and it is easy to become a prisoner of your worries. To create the life you want and be happy, you must take control and trust in your ability to try new approaches and find new ways to get where you are trying to go, literally or metaphorically. The freedom and ability to embrace one's power is what I call *creative confidence*, and guess what? You have it already.

Don't be alarmed if you don't think of yourself as a creative person. The word creative is often misunderstood as relating only to the arts. Everyone can tap in to their creativity—and have creative confidence—because the definition is simply "having the ability or power to create."[31]

> *Sue, a mother who had stayed home to raise her young children, needed assistance reentering the full-time work force and wanted to identify her natural talents. As we went over the results of her innate abilities test together, a common misunderstanding about creativity arose. Her test results indicated that she was a highly organized, scientific and detailed person who enjoyed problem solving and was very creative.*

---

31. 2006. *The American Heritage Dictionary of the English Language* (4th ed.). Boston, MA: Houghton Mifflin Company.

Sue said, "I never thought of myself as a creative person; I don't do any sort of art. I also thought that 'analytical' was the opposite of 'creative.'"

I explained that creativity has many outlets beyond artistic expression and that problem solving also is creative. She said, "I never thought of creativity that way. I guess I am creative!" She was excited, and her self-confidence was clearly boosted by this realization.

Using creative confidence involves imagining alternative courses of action, using the anticipation of new possibilities for your future to recharge your energy and then harnessing your innate power to make innovative choices. Your inner sage is the perfect companion for this task, because it knows what you really want and what you are capable of doing. In Step 2: Go Inward to Find Your Answers and Step 3: Design Your Ideal Life, consulting your inner sage was an important aspect of creating a big-picture vision of your ideal life (e.g., wanting to spend more time with loved ones) as well as day-to-day decision making (e.g., deciding to ask for time off). Consulting your inner sage with questions about both long-term planning and immediate situations will help you trust your ability to solve problems creatively.

One May, David E. Kelly—writer of many popular television programs such as The Practice, Ally McBeal, LA Law *and* Boston Legal*—gave the commencement address at his alma mater, Boston University Law School, where my good friend Elisabeth was graduating. He talked to the new graduates about choices, reminding them that even though it might look like they were heading down a predictable, unchangeable path of law firms and partnerships, it wasn't the only way.*

Kelly used his own experience to prove his point. He had always wanted to be a writer and had ultimately found an unusual way to combine his legal education with his passion for writing by creating television shows with legal themes. His inspirational speech urged everyone in the audience to discover what they want for their lives and to trust in their ability to create it. In essence, he advocated for each person to reject limited thinking and access their own creative confidence.

By recognizing limited thinking, then trusting yourself to be more creative, you can improve the quality of your decisions and thus your whole life. What's more, the journey toward your ideal life will be shorter when you allow yourself to consider, seek and create alternate pathways. Begin building your creative confidence by completing Exercise 34: Find a New Way. This small step will prepare you for making big changes later, as needed.

EXERCISE 34:
Find a New Way

For most people, the easiest way to go through life is status quo—that is, the way things are. Doing things the same way, time after time, feels familiar and doesn't require much effort or brain power.

Making dramatic life changes requires discovering and finding the confidence to try alternatives, because Plan A isn't always possible. Try your hand at creating some Plan Bs.

→ During the next seven days, pick at least one routine task that you always do the same way, and do it differently. Some suggestions include:

- Taking a different driving route or a different mode of transportation to work
- Delegating a household task to someone else in the household or hiring someone to do it for you
- Requesting delivery of something you usually pick up yourself
- Suggesting a barter arrangement in place of a paid service
- Doing your morning or evening routine in a different order

The possibilities are endless! Notice whether these different ways of achieving your objectives take more or less of your time or inspire you to find simpler and better ways to do other things as well.

Beyond Risk

Because making dramatic life changes necessarily involves taking risks, small and large, it is important to identify and address barriers to risk-taking behavior.

Fears and Assumptions

Achieving any goal—getting a better job, meeting a soul mate, eating a healthier diet, expressing a hidden talent or doing anything else that feels new—requires taking some sort of risk. Whether the alternate routes are big (like starting a new relationship) or small (like eating kale for the first time), you must find the courage to take the plunge.

I once led a telephone seminar for two hundred members of Executive Women International about having the courage to take risks. One of the most important things I told them was that when a person feels overwhelmed about the idea of taking a new risk, fear and limited thinking are often the cause.

Although fear comes in many forms, most prevalent is a fear of success or failure. People may avoid taking risks because this fear is related to potential shame or humiliation (e.g., "I'll look like a fool," "I'll be embarrassed" or "People will think I'm arrogant"). Instead, they keep the fear private, where it is not subject to objective scrutiny. Concealed fear grows and becomes more powerful; it's a vicious cycle which creates paralyzing and exhausting results.

The result is a fatigued brain unable to think clearly and distinguish truth from exaggeration. The reality is, fears are often overstated and unlikely to come to pass. Only when you can rest, step back and look at your fears objectively can you judge how valid they really are and take the appropriate action. To overcome an exaggerated fear, you must ask yourself, "What am I most afraid will happen if I fail?" After exposing your deepest fear, determine how realistic it is and make plans based on your best judgment of reality.

General, unfounded (not based on fact) assumptions, which really are imagined fears, can also hold people back and make them feel afraid to take action because they assume a negative outcome rather than a positive one.

For a long time, David had wanted to move into a higher-level position in his company. Because he always assumed that an advanced degree, which he doesn't have, would be required for that position, he has never applied.

After discussing his fears with me and realizing that his assumptions were unfounded, David approached the manager of human resources to ask what his options were, given his qualifications and experience. He learned that his extensive experience could substitute for an advanced degree and that he could apply for an upper-level position.

When you find yourself procrastinating about a decision or are too anxious to make a change, you may be being sidelined by overblown fears, limited thinking and unfounded assumptions. Complete Exercise 35: Find the Facts, Conquer Your Fear to learn how to overcome fears of success or failure, clear up assumptions, identify the real facts of the situation and find the courage to take a risk.

EXERCISE 35:

Find the Facts, Conquer Your Fear

To conquer your fear, you need courage. To bolster your courage, you need facts. The most effective way to identify the facts is with some unbiased assistance.

→ To begin, ask a supportive friend, partner, coach or colleague for help. Then, think about an area of your life or a situation that makes you feel unsure or fearful.

1. Explain to your partner all of the elements of the situation that you are unsure or fearful about. *(Speaking these details aloud to someone will help you differentiate the facts from the assumptions.)*

2. Your partner should listen carefully, then play devil's advocate to ensure that you have considered the situation from all possible angles, are clear about the facts and have not unwittingly jumped to any conclusions. If helpful, try using the questions and techniques from Exercise 16: Dissolve Your Fear in Step 2: Go Inward to Find Your Answers (page 86).

3. Together or alone, temporarily put aside all of your assumptions or test them using Exercise 19: Test Your Assumptions in Step 3: Design Your Ideal Life (page 103). Begin to identify creative alternatives on the basis of the facts alone.

Working with just the facts, you will feel more emotionally neutral and therefore more confident and courageous about moving forward.

Hesitation

Being reluctant to act quickly is another way people avoid taking risk. Change may present itself as opportunity, and opportunities have a way of coming unexpectedly.

If you find yourself hesitating when faced with a new opportunity, ask yourself this question to find your truth in the situation:

Has this desire been slow-burning; have I wanted to have or to do this for a long time?

Even though the *opportunity* may be new, your desire for it may not be. In fact, it may have been brewing for ages and you are more ready to take immediate action than you think.

For example, my client Peter used to teach art but had been unsuccessful in finding a teaching position since relocating close to family several years before. In the meantime, he was making a living selling commercial real estate, which he didn't enjoy, and longed to get back to teaching art. During our work together, an art teacher position opened up at a local school.

> *"The position sounds great, but I'm hesitant to do it because dropping my real estate works seems so impulsive," Peter said.*
>
> *"Are you kidding?" I replied. "This is exactly what you've been waiting years for!"*
>
> *I guess Peter needed some reminding. He took the leap, was offered the job and finally got back into the line of work that he loves.*

Most people are not in the habit of or are afraid of taking risks. But to create your ideal life, you must be willing to step up and take responsibility for your desires. Whether you want to try dating for the first time in years or move to a new city, you have the tools to turn risk into bliss. Take that leap, and trust that you can find your way. **Honoring yourself by living your ideal life is the only way to get what you really want.**

Complete Exercise 36: Take a Small Risk to increase your confidence in this area. Trust me; the rewards are worth it!

EXERCISE 36:
Take a Small Risk

Mahatma Gandhi is attributed with saying, "If you don't ask, you don't get." Sure, when you ask for something you risk the possibility of rejection (i.e., getting a negative reply). However, you also dramatically increase your chances of making forward progress toward your goals.

Here's a way to practice taking risks that won't be too difficult—and the results just might surprise you!

→ For the next two weeks, try asking friends, family and colleagues for things you normally wouldn't. Ignore any limited thinking that assumes their answers will be no. Ask for all kinds of things, like a morning off from work, help carrying the groceries or to have someone else drive for a change. If you feel brave, why not ask for larger things, like a raise or a weekend away?

Notice how many responses to your requests are yes and how many are no; simply keep count. Especially notice how often you are surprised to hear "Yes" to requests you previously wouldn't have thought to make. Remember that if you hadn't asked, you never could've gotten what you wanted.

Forward Motion

An alternate route around a traffic jam might take longer than the usual route. However, it might be an acceptable alternative if the driver continues to move forward, remaining in control of their destiny, moving closer to their destination and maybe—just maybe—beating the vehicles that remain stuck in the bottleneck. The same is true of obstacles you face as you make dramatic life changes. Remember that big life changes result from a steady pace of small advances, not by getting everything done at once (as discussed in Getting There, One Step at a Time in Step 3: Design Your Ideal Life, page 139)! Even if the road feels unfamiliar, as long as you continue to make consistent progress, you will stay motivated, energized and creative—three essential characteristics of a person who is successful in making dramatic and permanent life change.

To recognize the effectiveness of taking small, consistent actions, all you need to do is look back at your own life and take inventory of how far you have come already.

Complete Exercise 37: Remind Yourself of Successes to recall past achievements and build your confidence for making more life changes, one small step at a time.

EXERCISE 37:

Remind Yourself of Successes

When you look back at what you have already accomplished (events, activities and accolades), you will realize that you can learn to swim, earn a degree or climb a mountain by taking small steps. The keys are getting started, staying motivated and pacing yourself!

→ Start by recalling one of the proudest moments of your life. To find one quickly, turn back to your answers for Exercise 22: Create Goals (for Each Facet) for the first facet you worked on in Step 3: Design Your Ideal Life.

1. Copy the most important accomplishment from your answers to question #6 ("At this point in my life, what three accomplishments related to this facet am I most proud of?") to a new page in your YOLO journal.

2. List as many steps as you can remember that led to this accomplishment.

3. List the three strongest personality traits that helped you achieve this accomplishment. *(If you can, also pose this question to people who were close to you as you worked toward and reached this goal. They may remember details that you have forgotten!)*

4. List any external support or resources that helped you achieve this accomplishment.

5. Determine how long it took to reach your goal from start to finish. Was it longer or shorter than you might have thought?

The information that you have revealed in this exercise demonstrates that you can indeed make big changes; you have done it before. As you move toward your vision of your ideal life,

- **Seek out the kinds of support and resources that have helped you in the past.**
- **Use your strongest personality traits to help you achieve your goals.**
- **Have patience with your progress. The end result will be well worth the wait.**

If you want to bolster your confidence even more, repeat this exercise with another accomplishment from your answers to question #6 in Exercise 22: Create Goals (for Each Facet), for the same facet or a different one. Then return to this exercise whenever you need a little ego boost!

A New Perspective

Nothing would be done at all if a man waited until he could do it so well that no one could find fault with it.

–Cardinal Newman

One of the important benefits of slowing down is the ability to make much better decisions more easily, in a calm frame of mind. It completely changes a person's view of the world. Sometimes the best way to break out of limited thinking and access creative confidence is to consciously change perspective.

The next time you are feeling so afraid, overwhelmed and in the grips of limited thinking that you're unable to think clearly, take a break and reevaluate.

Walk away and take some deep breaths, then ask your inner sage whether you are putting too much importance where it doesn't belong. Your break can be as simple as a short walk or as involved as a vacation. Just try to temporarily remove yourself from the situation that makes you feel stuck.

One March, I took a weekend break that did wonders for my perspective, which had begun to stray from my definition of lifespan productivity.

Being a leisurely tourist on a last-minute getaway was in sharp contrast to my work life in the preceding days! When I started to relax, I realized how stressful my life had become. Before the trip, I had been feeling overwhelmed, worrying about getting out marketing pieces and making many business-related decisions. My fuse had been shorter than usual. I hadn't been making enough time for self-care, healthy eating or coasting.

After the weekend away, I was solidly back on my feet, feeling totally different—creative and refreshed. I had a clearer perspective and a longer fuse. I was able to break free from my fears that projects would not pan out the way I had wanted, and to escape my limited thinking that there was only one way—often the hard way—to get things done. I was also able to see that I had made the outcomes of my work projects more important than they really were and more important than my quality of life; I consequently made some much-needed adjustments to my priorities.

It is critical to recognize that in any situation **you have multiple options, and you have the power to determine the importance placed on each option.** Therefore, the level of pressure or stress you allow yourself to experience is also within your power to control. Challenges present many opportunities to think creatively and have many possible "correct" solutions; no single one is necessarily better than the others. When you apply your personal creativity, rest assured that you will find the best solution for you and your situation.

The trick to seeing those multiple options is to shift your perspective. Step back, look at the situation objectively and ask yourself whether you might be caught up in limited thinking or in society's standards instead of your own. The three best ways to do that are to slow down by coasting (Step 1: Put "Enjoy Life" Back on the Agenda), consult your inner sage (Step 2: Go Inward to Find Your Answers) and simply take a break.

Helpful Hints

When building your confidence and transforming your vision into reality, you challenge the status quo and rock the boat for everyone around you. No matter what others might think, say or do, remember that you are pursuing *your* ideal life and nobody else's.

Surround yourself with loving, helpful supporters who infuse you with positive energy, particularly those who have already made life-improving changes. At the same time, be prepared to accept that some family, friends and colleagues may not be supportive of your plan if it makes them feel insecure or uncomfortable.

Be selective in the people you turn to for support, because advice from other people may be clouded by their own fear-based, limited thinking. In other words, they might think about what your risk-taking decision implies for them, not for you. For example, a friend who is jealous of an opportunity that has come your way and wishes he had the courage to make similar changes in his life might let his beliefs and fears come forth in negative outbursts such as, "You're crazy for doing that!" or "What makes you think you'll be successful?" as a defense mechanism.

Remind yourself that you are creative, supported and resourceful … and continue to take small steps toward your goals. Don't let yourself get stuck in "it's impossible" or "there's no way" thinking. There *is* a way. It *is* possible. When you recognize limited thinking, slow down and take a break. To combat negative thoughts, repeat such statements as, "I am creating a new life for myself," "I can reach my goals" and "I am proud of the lifespan-productive decisions that I make." Then tap in to your creative confidence to find the alternative solution that will keep you moving forward.

The reality is this: **You are in control of every aspect of your life.** You are ultimately responsible for all of your successes as well as all the areas of your life in which you feel unsuccessful. The good news is that you are also the only one who can change any of it—and you are already well on your way to living the new life you want simply by having worked your way through the five-step YOLO program. Well done!

The next and final chapter, Make Your Way in the Real World, offers ways to stay motivated and maintain your momentum as you take your newfound knowledge and power out into the real world.

Make Your Way in the Real World

TRANSLATING A VISION INTO ACTION CAN BE DAUNTING WHEN MANY ASPECTS OF LIFE ARE CHANGING! LEARN HOW TO STAY MOTIVATED AND ON TRACK TOWARD YOUR GOALS AS YOUR JOURNEY EVOLVES.

It's no use saying we are doing our best. You have to succeed in doing what is necessary.

~WINSTON CHURCHILL

Term Used in This Chapter

vision markers: signs that provide positive (or negative) reinforcement that one's actions are in line with their ideals (or not); may take the form of success, failure, unexpected help or surprising coincidence

Congratulations! You have taken five giant steps toward dramatically changing your life by:

- Slowing down and coasting, appreciating and creating moments of happiness, and putting enjoyment back on your daily agenda (Step 1: Put "Enjoy Life" Back on the Agenda).
- Consulting your inner sage for wisdom and guidance (Step 2: Go Inward to Find Your Answers).
- Describing your ideals for the Ten Facets of Your Ideal Life, creating facet goals and a plan for achieving them, and clarifying your vision for your ideal life (Step 3: Design Your Ideal Life).
- Abandoning society's notion of *productivity* and instead learning to judge your life's success on your own terms (Step 4: Redefine What It Means to Be Productive).
- Learning how to build a support network, approach obstacles with confidence and creativity, and conquer your fears (Step 5: Build Your Self-Confidence).

Still, you probably can think of a half a dozen reasons why you *really can't* put these techniques into practice right now, from a less-than-ideal economy to unsupportive loved ones. Planning to make dramatic life changes is one thing; taking your newfound knowledge and techniques out into the real world is another! The thing is, how you address real-world distractions is *your* choice. You can allow them to derail you from your path or provide you with opportunities for self-investigation and creative strategy.

One powerful reality that you must remember is this: **You are solely responsible for making progress (or not!) toward your vision of your ideal life.** Just as no one else can dream your dreams for you, no one else can create your ideal life, either.

You have made too much progress to stop now. Use the momentum you feel from reading this book and working your way through the You Only Live Once (YOLO) program to continue to make real life changes. This chapter will teach you how to remain connected to your vision of your ideal life (which may change over time, and that's okay!), stay on track toward your goals and recognize signs of support for your efforts, wherever they may be.

Continued Motivation

Half an hour's meditation is essential except when you are very busy. Then a full hour is needed.

-Saint Francis de Sales

Everyone's motivation level varies over time. This cycle is completely normal and an expected part of the life-improvement process.

Some days you will feel like anything is possible! Other days you will feel like the universe is against you, when external factors (like a demanding boss) or internal factors (like fear and self-doubt) present obstacles to your progress. Know that all obstacles are temporary. Expect them and recognize them for what they are—bumps in the road, not dead ends—and you will have the conviction, creativity and ability to continue moving toward your goals.

A few ways to remind yourself of the importance of your task and regain your waning motivation follow. And don't forget to ask for help from your supporters if you need it!

Empowerment

Making dramatic life changes requires great courage. **Remind yourself of your vision of your ideal life to draw the strength you need to face the world and have the faith to continue moving toward your goals.** And give yourself credit where it is due.

Don't get caught in a trap that will lead you back to where you were before you started reading this book! Giving in to the temptation to settle for less is a sure path back to dissatisfaction, frustration and stress. Your state of mind will make the difference on this journey, so take conscious measures to maintain your focus: Slow down, coast, revisit your notes, repeat the exercises, make consistent progress and reward yourself along the way.

Positive Thinking

When faced with difficulty, remind yourself that everything in nature is cyclical; there is a natural rise and fall of events. Even if you feel discouraged, trust that if you use your creative confidence and continue to move toward your goals *anyway*, the road will always rise back up to meet you. **Keep taking consistent, small, positive actions to stay connected to your vision of your ideal life and maintain your motivation.** If you allow your mind to focus on the negative (what you don't have and what isn't working) instead, you will lose valuable opportunities for creativity, growth and progress.

Inspiration

Look to your inner sage regularly for inspiration, as you learned in Step 2: Go Inward to Find Your Answers. Remind yourself often of the importance of your journey and your goals: Post motivating pictures, objects, signs and sayings around your home or office, and send yourself daily, weekly or monthly reminders (photos, notes, sayings, quotes and so on) using online calendars and other electronic reminder tools. Download motivational YOLO posters from my website www.youonlyliveoncebook.com. Ask your supporters to periodically check in with you, too.

Share your vision with others to keep it alive and healthy. **The more you share your vision, the bigger and stronger it will grow—and the faster you will progress toward it.** Invigorated by your progress, you will be healthier, more focused and more available for relationships. What's more, the people who love you will recognize the positive changes in you and be happy along with you, because enthusiasm for life is contagious. Not surprisingly, many clients have come to me because they were inspired to dramatically change their lives after watching a friend, colleague or family member "come alive" while working the five-step YOLO process. Who might you inspire?

Like all the real people illustrated in this book, you *can* improve your life. When you feel doubtful, remember everyone who has been down this path before you and succeeded in achieving their goals. The world *needs* more focused, happy people who are enjoying their ideal lives rather than people who feel disconnected or exhausted due to their stressful lifestyles. In becoming a focused, happy person yourself, you surely will have a positive effect on many people around you.

Mike was an unfulfilled Ph.D. biologist in an impressive position at the Massachusetts Institute of Technology. After working with me as his life coach, he said, "Before going through this process, I was always finding ways to hide. I was not truly engaged and part of my environment. Now, I see a direction for my life and that I am in control."

He says he used to think, "If I just went along, something would happen and things would work out. It was a nebulous, passive approach to my career and, ultimately, my life." Changing his mind-set to "believing anything is possible" was the essential step that led Mike to make a dramatic career change from academia to the legal field. After that shift, he felt free to pursue his personal goals of starting a family with his wife and owning a home.

With increased self-knowledge and self-confidence, Mike achieved two out of three of his goals in just over a year and continues to work toward the third. "Now I feel that I can always change my situation. It never hurts to ask for help or try something. A mix of perseverance, creativity, hard work and willingness to listen can get you to where you want to go and, quite possibly, somewhere even better."

Resolve

No matter how committed a person is at the start of a new undertaking, distractions and temptations to stray from the chosen path are to be expected. Being prepared to counter them with a strong resolve is the best way to stay true to yourself and your commitment.

Some distractions are internal—doubts and fears disguised as a voice of reason or a devil's advocate. You might ask yourself, "Is all this effort really worth it?" or "Do I really want to think about my life this much?" And you might even find yourself thinking, "My old way of living wasn't so bad. Some days were better than others, but on the whole things were okay—right?" Well, yes, yes—and probably not.

Other distractions are external and may even be so common as to be predictable. For example, many of my clients have experienced temptation, just before taking a significant new step toward their ideal life, in the form of an opportunity—often involving money—that they would have considered attractive before, but is *no longer* in line with their vision. Their commitment is tested by having to choose between their new vision of their ideal life and something that previously would have been appealing.

Mary, a freelance editor, began planning a two-week trip to South America to try out her dream of living in another country. Just as she was booking her travel, she was offered two high-paying work projects that would have prevented her trip. It was extremely difficult to turn down the needed income, but Mary knew the test trip was important to her long-term vision, so she went anyway.

Mary's journey was such a huge success that a few months later she was living and working in Buenos Aires, Argentina, and is still there now. If she had taken those tempting projects, her dream would have been delayed, temporarily or permanently.

Temptations that are seemingly too good to pass up can serve an important purpose, providing the opportunity for you to affirm or deny your commitment to your new path. If you affirm your commitment, your sacrifice allows you to become more invested in your vision. If you deny your commitment, you need to reexamine your true desires and dispel any fears that may be holding you back. I can't explain why this phenomenon occurs with so many clients, but you should be prepared to call on the strength of your convictions to resist it.

Colm is a wonderful example of someone who stayed connected to a vision with empowerment, positive thinking, inspiration and resolve. A few years ago, he made a dramatic life change to pursue his dream of climbing mountains.

When asked about his future and leaving his position as a senior technical representative for a highly respected commercial roofing company, Colm answered confidently that he knew exactly what he was doing. "I am prepared. I have been planning for this. I am going to do this now, while I am young enough and physically able, and when I'm done, I'll find a way to combine my love of the outdoors with a workable career." He methodically researched and then attended several advanced alpine climbing schools in Denali National

Park in Alaska and Mount Rainer National Park in Washington State, then lived in the mountains doing what he loved for another year.

After Colm had achieved his mountain-climbing dream, he met a wonderful woman who shares his love of the outdoors, and they moved to rural New Hampshire. He returned to his career rejuvenated and ready for the next adventure. Before long he found a new position in his field which allowed him a flexible schedule so he could continue to enjoy his love of being outdoors.

Colm was in touch with a wellspring of conviction that moved him to take action toward his goals while others around him were still dreaming of theirs.

Complete Exercise 38: Do a Reality Check to remind yourself why you started the YOLO process and help you stay motivated. Then, complete Exercise 39: Test Your Plan to determine whether your actions are in line with your vision.

EXERCISE 38:
Do a Reality Check

Something made you read this book. Recall exactly what it was that brought you to this point. Were you unhappy for a long time? Were you bored at or laid off from your job? Had you recently ended or were you considering ending a close relationship?

→ In your YOLO journal, list the areas of your life that you had wished to change, leaving some space between each entry. Taking one item at a time, answer the following questions:

1. **How do I feel about that situation now?**
2. **Has the situation changed at all?**

3. **Have I set goals to make it change?**

4. **Have I taken action on my goals in this area of my life?**

If you are feeling good about your progress, congratulations—you're working the YOLO program! If not, you need to stop and reassess your situation. Reconnect with your vision of your ideal life (Exercise 24: Clarify Your Vision, page 140), create goals, determine your first action toward your goals and schedule it on your calendar within the next four weeks.

Note: Under certain rare circumstances, immediate changes in a particular area may not be the best plan for improving your life right now. A short-term wait may be more appropriate. If your path forward in a particular area of your life isn't clearly marked by now, ask yourself,

5. **Is there any reason I would choose not to make changes to improve this area of my life right now?** ***(For example, you might want to move to a new locale but not uproot your children part-way through the school year; you might want to change jobs but expect to receive a bonus soon; or you might plan to get divorced but haven't yet worked out the financial details.)***

6. **If so, what circumstances need to change in order for me to move forward?** ***(For example, it might make sense to wait until the end of the school year before moving, delay your change of employment until after the end of the bonus period, or get your financial house in order before filing divorce papers.)***

If you find yourself in this kind of situation, think about how you can expedite these changes (i.e., your answers to question #6) so you can move toward your goals and achieve your vision of your ideal life. Determine what your first action will be once circumstances allow, and schedule it on your calendar.

EXERCISE 39:

Test Your Plan

To maintain motivation and momentum as you move toward your goals, verify that your action items are in line with your vision of your ideal life. This quick exercise can help.

→ Find a quiet space to consult your YOLO journal. Review your answers to Exercise 25: Organize Your Action Items. Think about one action that you plan to take toward creating your ideal life. Ask your inner sage,

"How do I honestly feel, deep down, about the potential outcomes of this action? Excited? Relieved? Scared? A combination of these feelings?"

Excitement is a strong indicator that this action item is in line with your vision.

A sense of relief—like a burden has been lifted from your shoulders—indicates that this action item definitely is in line with your vision.

Fear or dread—extreme fear, a negative intuition a lot stronger than just butterflies in your stomach—indicates that you intend to make this change for the wrong reasons and that this action item is not truly supportive of your vision.

Nervous excitement about a change—feeling both excited or relieved and a bit scared is normal. It also is a good indicator that this action item is in line with your vision.

If you feel excitement, relief or nervous excitement, proceed with your action item, because it is the right thing to do. However, if you feel dread, do not proceed. Take some time to talk with a trusted friend, partner, life coach or close colleague and uncover the true motivation behind your intended action. What you learn from this situation can help you avoid it in the future.

Repeat this exercise for any action item on your list for Exercise 25: Organize Your Action Items, and whenever you need to determine whether your plan is in line with your vision. And remember, don't proceed with an action unless you feel excitement, relief or nervous excitement about it, because only those feelings signal an alignment with your vision of your ideal life.

The Path to Your Future

Faith is necessary to victory.

–William Hazlett

Every person has a unique purpose or calling that they are meant to attain, and it is reached by traveling a safe, clearly marked (for those who know how to recognize it) route extending from here and now to the future. People who use their natural talents, live according to their personal values, feel passionate about and fulfilled by what they choose to do, and pursue lifespan-productive activities are living their life's purpose.

By completing the YOLO program and working toward being true to yourself and your vision for all Ten Facets of Your Ideal Life (summarized in your answers to Exercise 24: Clarify Your Vision), you have found your intended path, and the universe will support your efforts; the road ahead will be straight and smooth. When you forget to take breaks from your mental agenda, revert to society's definition of *productivity* or fall victim to limited thinking and false priorities, you compromise your ideals and wander off the path, unsupported; the road will become winding and rough. Remembering to coast, staying connected to your vision, and engaging the support of others will help you stay on—or return to—your path.

Many people are unaware of signs from the universe that are clues about whether their actions are in line with their ideals. I call all of these signs—which may take the form of success or failure, unexpected help or obstacles, or good or bad luck—*vision markers*. This concept may sound a bit "out there" to some of you, so let me explain where I am coming from. As a spiritual, but not religious person, I take inspiration from many sources, including nature, friends, my inner sage (of course!) and the fundamental lessons that have been passed down from compassionate and wise leaders from all cultures throughout human history. My perspective on signs that emanate from the universe comes from personal experience. I first noticed them when I started making dramatic changes in my own life and have since witnessed them occurring in my clients' lives as well. Over the years, I have come to regard and rely on vision markers as important sign posts in my coaching work as well as in my personal life.

Vision markers may be attributed to destiny, serendipity, divine influence, God, the law of attraction or something else altogether. Whatever your belief, **vision markers are evidence of a universal support or lack of support for your choices that can encourage you to pursue your vision with confidence or to reconsider your direction.**

Universal Support

Have you ever noticed that when you are in a groove, accomplishing something important to you, the universe seems to be on your side—traffic lights turn green as you approach, money appears in your pocket or someone comes into your life who can help you do exactly what you are trying to do? These helpful coincidences are not random.

Some people say that thought brings about action. I agree. When you focus your thoughts, energy and actions on something, the universe responds in kind. In other words, what you put out, you get back—both positive and negative. So when you harness this phenomenon by keeping your thoughts positive and actively pursuing what you truly, deeply desire (following the five-step YOLO program!), the correct path shows itself in subtle—or not-so-subtle—ways.

I have observed this universal support appear over and over again for my clients when they set their course in the direction of what they truly want. For example:

- *Shortly after Gary (the French horn player from Step 3: Design Your Ideal Life) decided to leave his comfortable-but-stressful job as a certified public accountant, his company offered all employees a voluntary separation package. Gary accepted this ideal offer immediately and used it to explore his talents and develop a road map for his life. Similarly, after Gary decided to move to San Francisco, his house in Philadelphia sold immediately, he was offered an interim place to live and he found a well-paid consulting arrangement with just a few phone calls. Furthermore, Gary has been offered numerous opportunities to play French horn with orchestras he'd never thought possible. Though it certainly took effort and ongoing courage to change his life in so many ways, Gary felt that the transitions were smooth, as if he was doing exactly what he was supposed to be doing.*

- *Kate (the former software engineer from Step 2: Go Inward to Find Your Answers who created a new career for herself working with a manufacturer of artificial hearts) had a long-term live-in boyfriend, but she longed for a more committed relationship. Because she had tapped in to the powerful force of her creative confidence when she changed careers, she was able to find the strength to end the unfulfilling relationship once and for all. And not long after she did, she found a new boyfriend. They married and now have a daughter.*

- *For more than fifteen years, my friend John had a dream of moving from London to America, but events never seemed to line up properly. While vacationing in the United States recently, his dream was clarified and invigorated. He returned to London excited and did an Internet search for U.S.-based jobs in his field of lighting design—a specialized industry. Miraculously, he found a perfect fit in Boston—exactly where he wanted to relocate.*

- *When I fully embraced my vision of writing this book, I started to experience abundant support for my decision. A group of local coaches (people I had only met once!) generously offered to read chapters and give me feedback, a local woman told me she had a background in doing publicity for books and would love to help me, a new friend introduced me to a freelance editor who had worked on self-help books in the past and was looking for new clients, I went to a lecture and sat next to a stranger who ended up being the perfect portrait photographer to take the photograph of me you see on this book ... the list goes on and on.*

It doesn't matter what you call these fortuitous signs. You don't even have to believe in them. However, **recognizing vision markers as the indicators they are can increase your confidence, boost your energy and help you maintain momentum.** Complete Exercise 40: Notice Positive Vision Markers to begin seeing signs in your life that reinforce your decision-making.

EXERCISE 40:
Notice Positive Vision Markers

When you are on the true path to your goals, events occur with effort, but the progress is smooth, not forced.

→ Take a moment to think back over the last year and recall times you have noticed vision markers—yours or anyone else's. Record them in your YOLO journal. Some questions to jog your memory include the following:

1. Have I had a streak of good luck? Bad luck?
2. Have any quirky coincidences or twists of fate become my favorite stories to tell?
3. Does someone I know have a tale about a just-in-time good fortune that saved the day?
4. Have I met someone for whom things always seem to go his or her way? If so, do I think that person is living in line with their vision of an ideal life?

For the next week or so, pay attention to vision markers as they appear around you. Be aware of little coincidences that other people mention, too.

Barriers in All Directions

The opposite of universal support feels like a universal "No." Every effort seems to lead to a dead end (e.g., you can't find the critical information you seek, or a supplier is always closed when you are able to get there). Discouraging obstacles that present themselves are vision markers, too—signs indicating a problem with your efforts that needs to be addressed. They may represent lessons to be learned (e.g., to slow down even more) or the need for a potentially uncomfortable change of direction. Heeding the signs will bring you back to the path that leads to your ideal life. If you have ever given up on a particularly difficult, frustrating project in favor of another option, only to discover that it is better and easier, you have already experienced—and responded to—such vision markers!

When you feel that nothing is going right, clarify and redefine your path by revisiting how your vision, your goals and your actions are correlated. Complete Exercise 41: Address Negative Vision Markers to identify how you might have lost track of your vision and what to do to get yourself back on the right path toward your goals.

EXERCISE 41:

Address Negative Vision Markers

When you are trying to take action but feel stuck and frustrated by negative vision markers, it's important to examine the situation and choose appropriate alternative actions that will help you make forward progress instead.

→ To begin, recall a situation in which you were trying to achieve a goal but barriers prevented your every move, or your efforts did not produce the desired results. Find a quiet, comfortable place to have a focused conversation with your inner sage. Imagine that you're still in that frustrating situation, hearing the universal "No" at every turn, and ask yourself the following questions. Record your answers in your YOLO journal.

1. **Am I following my vision of my ideal life? (Reread your answers to Exercise 24: Clarify Your Vision for a refresher.)**

2. **Am I ignoring a basic need (food, shelter or safety) that requires immediate attention?**

3. **Do I have a fear that needs to be addressed?**

4. **What do I really want right now?**

5. **How is this goal out of alignment with my answers to questions #1 through #4? Could I modify my goal to bring it into alignment? If so, how?**

6. **What steps can I take to prepare myself to move toward my goal?** ***(For instance, it may be necessary to get back in touch with your vision, ensure that your basic needs are met and overcome unaddressed fears. For additional guidance, reread the note about rare circumstances in Exercise 38: Do a Reality Check (page 208), and complete questions #5 and #6 from that exercise, if appropriate. Also, return to Exercise 16: Dissolve Your Fear in Step 2: Go Inward to Find Your Answers (page 86) and Exercise 19: Test Your Assumptions in Step 3: Design Your Ideal Life (page 103) and do them again with your specific frustration in mind. The results from these exercises should give you the clarity and direction you need to move forward.)***

Repeat this exercise whenever you are trying to take action but feel stuck and frustrated by negative vision markers.

Helpful Hints

This book has given you the opportunity to break out of stress overload and reclaim your quality of life. Going forward, it will be important to continue to protect the things that are most important to you—your physical health, mental well-being, passions and relationships—as your ideal life evolves.

To live your ideal life, you must:

- Stay empowered to follow your vision and move toward your goals, avoiding the temptation to fall backward.
- Rely on your personal YOLO support network.
- Maintain your momentum, confidence and motivation while traveling along your path.

A few simple suggestions should help you stay on track.

Continue to take immediate action toward your vision to ensure that you mentally and physically break free from your old life. Avoid the temptation to close this book and just think about it. The initial rush of motivation fades quickly if not maintained, and the longer you pause, the more vulnerable to disillusion you become. Before you know it, you'll find yourself back where you were before you read this book. In completing the five-step YOLO program, you have already created the plan that will allow you to achieve your ideal life. Follow through with additional action to continue the momentum you've already created. So today, while your creativity and motivation are high:

- Pick up the phone, call someone who will support your journey and share one or two of your most exciting facet goals.

- Select at least one initial action item related to your facet goals that you can complete *during the next twenty-four hours,* and commit to doing it by writing it on your calendar or making a verbal commitment to one of your supporters.

Schedule a weekly or at least monthly check-in with your inner sage. Use this time to contemplate your progress and create your next action steps. It will help keep your momentum up and your pace on track toward your goals. Your happiness is a worthwhile pursuit, and it deserves a place in your appointment book.

Keep this book on your bookshelf and refer to its exercises time and again. Use it as an annual review, perhaps on your birthday or at the beginning of each new year. Every time you revisit these pages and do the exercises anew, you will uncover information and insights about yourself that will help you continue to create your ideal life, even as your vision changes.

Envision not only the ultimate outcome of your ideal life for you but also the ripple effect that you will cause! As you create the life you want, the people around you will be inspired by your newfound happiness, positive energy, increased clarity and enhanced creativity.

Money and possessions come and go. Even relationships wax and wane over the years. Time is the only finite resource. It is the only aspect of life that is truly and undeniably limited, because humans are, after all, mortal.

Need I say it? You only live once. As you continue to live the rest of your years, time will slowly tick away. Creating a life you love is the most worthwhile gift you can give to yourself and to those closest to you.

With the five steps you have learned in this book, you have created a path to the life you want. Now go live it!

ABOUT THE AUTHOR

Deirdre M. McEachern is a former software industry executive turned award-winning life coach, author and speaker. Using her unique You Only Live Once coaching program, she has helped thousands of individuals around the globe create lives that they love.

A graduate of Coach University, Deirdre also is credentialed as a Master Certified Coach by the International Federation of Coaches. She received a master's degree in peace studies from Trinity College in Dublin, Ireland, and was an adjunct professor of sociology at Emerson College in Boston, Massachusetts.

Deirdre, her husband and their children live in a historic farmhouse on the coast of Maine.

BIBLIOGRAPHY

Anderson, Virginia. 2003. "Too Much to Do." *Atlanta Journal-Constitution,* Nov. 18.

Arias, Elizabeth. United States Life Tables, 2000. *National Vital Statistics Reports* 2002: Vol. 51, No. 3, p. 33. www.cdc.gov/nchs/data/nvsr/nvsr51/nvsr51_03.pdf

Bolles, Richard Nelson. 2009. *What Color Is Your Parachute? A Practical Manual for Job-Hunters and Career-Changers.* Berkeley, CA: Ten Speed Press.

Bond, Michael. 2003. "The Pursuit of Happiness." *New Scientist,* Oct. 4.

Cameron, Julia. 2002. *The Artist's Way: A Spiritual Path to Higher Creativity* (10th anniversary ed.). New York: J. P. Tarcher/Putnam.

Center for the New American Dream. 2004. *Take Back Your Time Poll: Americans Eager to Take Back Their Time.* Charlottesville, VA: Center for the New American Dream. www.newdream.org/about/polls/timepoll.php

de Graaf, John, David Wann, and Thomas H. Naylor in association with Redefining Progress. 2001. *Affluenza: The All-Consuming Epidemic* (1st edition). San Francisco, CA: Berrett-Koehler Publishers.

de Graaf, John. no date. *Short on Time? Take Yours Back!* www.newdream.org/newsletter/tbytd.php, accessed Jan. 15, 2004.

Dominguez, Joe, and Vicki Robin. 1992. *Your Money or Your Life: Transforming Your Relationship with Money and Achieving Financial Independence.* New York: Viking.

Donovan, Nick, and David Halpern, with Richard Sargeant. 2002. *Life Satisfaction: The State of Knowledge and Implications for Government.* London, UK: Cabinet Office Strategy Unit, December. www.cabinetoffice.gov.uk/media/cabinetoffice/strategy/assets/paper.pdf

Hansen, Mark Victor, and Robert G. Allen. 2002. *The One Minute Millionaire: The Enlightened Way to Wealth* (1st edition). New York: Harmony Books.

Hutcheson, Don, and Bob McDonald. 2000. *Don't Waste Your Talent: The 8 Critical Steps to Discovering What You Do Best.* Atlanta, GA: Longstreet Press.

Jones, Clayton. 2010. Gallup Poll: Degree of One's Charity Depends on Happiness More Than Wealth. *Christian Science Monitor*'s Editorial Board blog, Sept. 10. www.csmonitor.com/Commentary/Editorial-Board-Blog/2010/0910/Gallup-poll-Degree-of-one-s-charity-depends-on-happiness-more-than-wealth

Miller, Kay. 2003. America's Compulsive Consumption. *Minneapolis–St. Paul Star Tribune,* reprinted in *Portsmouth Herald*, Dec. 14, p. F1.

Morgenstern, Julie. 2004. *Organizing from the Inside Out: The Foolproof System for Organizing Your Home, Your Office, and Your Life* (2nd ed.). New York: Henry Holt.

Mundis, Jerrold. 2003. *How to Get Out of Debt, Stay Out of Debt and Live Prosperously.* New York: Bantam Books.

Orman, Suzy. 2006. *The 9 Steps to Financial Freedom: Practical and Spiritual Steps So You Can Stop Worrying* (updated and revised 3rd edition). New York: Three Rivers Press.

Perlow, Leslie A., and Jessica L. Porter. 2009. Making Time Off Predictable—and Required. *Harvard Business Review,* Vol. 87, No. 10, pp. 102–109.

Rinzler, Carol Ann. 2006. *Nutrition for Dummies* (4th ed.). Indianapolis, IN: Wiley.

Roizen, Michael F., and Mehmet C. Oz, with Ted Spiker, Lisa Oz, and Craig Wynett. 2009. *YOU: On a Diet—The Owner's Manual for Waist Management* (revised, updated ed.). New York: Free Press.

Roth, Geneen. 2010. *Women Food and God: An Unexpected Path to Almost Everything*. New York: Simon & Schuster.

Winter, Barbara J. 2009. *Making a Living Without a Job: Winning Ways for Creating Work That You Love* (revised edition). New York: Bantam Books.

ONLINE RESOURCES

The Artist's Way Online	www.theartistsway.com
Discover Meditation (Pragito Dove)	www.discovermeditation.com
FlyLady	www.flylady.net
Google Groups	groups.google.com
Highland's Natural Ability Battery	www.highlandsco.com
Life Experience Inventory	www.vip-coaching.com
Meetup	www.meetup.com
Take Back Your Time Day	www.timeday.org
The Daily Plate	www.thedailyplate.com
Work to Live (Joe Robinson)	www.worktolive.info
Yahoo! Groups	groups.yahoo.com
You Only Live Once program and book	www.youonlyliveoncebook.com

8487615R0

Made in the USA
Charleston, SC
14 June 2011